TWENTIETH CENTURY INTERPRETATIONS
OF
THE RAINBOW

A Collection of Critical Essays

Edited by

MARK KINKEAD-WEEKES

Prentice-Hall, Inc. *Englewood Cliffs, N. J.*

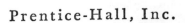

Quotations from *The Rainbow* by D. H. Lawrence, copyright 1915 by David Herbert Lawrence, renewed 1943 by Frieda Lawrence, are used by permission of The Viking Press, Inc., Laurence Pollinger, Ltd., and the Estate of the Late Mrs. Frieda Lawrence.

Current printing (last number):

10 9 8 7 6 5 4 3 2 1

PRENTICE-HALL INTERNATIONAL, INC. (*London*)
PRENTICE-HALL OF AUSTRALIA, PTY. LTD. (*Sydney*)
PRENTICE-HALL OF CANADA, LTD. (*Toronto*)
PRENTICE-HALL OF INDIA PRIVATE LIMITED (*New Delhi*)
PRENTICE-HALL OF JAPAN, INC. (*Tokyo*)

Contents

Introduction

by Mark Kinkead-Weekes

Poised between the very different worlds of *Sons and Lovers* and *Women in Love*, *The Rainbow* was a turning point for Lawrence in several ways.

His departure from England with Frieda in 1912 marked the end of that period of his life of which *Sons and Lovers* is the main achievement, and also the diagnosis. To write the novel he had to come to terms with himself and with the private malaise of his dependence on his mother; his relationship with Frieda made this possible. He was able to recast the autobiographical story that he had entitled "Paul Morel" and make art out of the pain of his past, because now it was over, and he felt himself a new man. The story of the struggles and the success of his marriage is told in the collection of poems he called *Look! We have come through*, and it was because he had "come through" that he could hope to understand and give shape to the tract of vitality and pain that lay behind.

The Rainbow was conceived and largely drafted in Italy, in the happiness of success, and in the last eighteen months of peace before August 1914. It was the first work of the new man free of his past; and the new kind of art he developed was directly connected in his mind with the change in himself that had come from being married. *The Rainbow* is a study of marriage before it is anything else. And although its final version (written in late 1914 and early 1915) reflects the impact of war, it does so in a rather special sense. For Lawrence's response to the outbreak of destruction was an urgent formulation and development of his deepest faith in creativity, especially the creativity inherent in the true relation of man and woman—"philosophically" in the *Study of Thomas Hardy*, and then more deeply and richly in the final version of *The Rainbow*. Though he worked hard to achieve the novel, it became a work of great confidence, bringing together his essentially religious sensibility and his new insight into both conflict and consummation in marriage. Though it ends in near disaster, it was originally intended as the first part of a saga of coming through. The autobiographical world of *Sons and Lovers*, the investigation into the self in a particular place and time, has given way to a confident historic sweep, an attempt to plot the inner history of a changing England over three generations from the mid-nineteenth to the early twentieth century. The new "metaphysical" foundation has universalized the point of view; and despite its investigations of pains, failures, and destructive urges, the novel is ultimately celebratory. Indeed, Lawrence saw it as a sacred history in which the workings of divinely creative forces could be detected within the relationship of men and women, founded in conflict, thwarted by human failure, but still available, covenanted.

Only five weeks after publication, the publishers withdrew the novel because the Bow Street Magistrate's Court held it to be obscene. Through 1915 and 1916, as the pattern of trench war hardened and the toll of casualties mounted towards the terrible climax of the Somme, the faith of *The Rainbow* gave way to a grimmer apocalyptic vision of a world dominated by urges of death and destruction. In his tiny cottage in Cornwall, beset by the suspicion and dislike of the local people for the bearded outsider and his German wife, Lawrence began what was to have been the continuation of *The Rainbow* in a mood of hatred for a "putrescent mankind." After what had happened to his book he felt he no longer had a public: the idea of "Rananim," the small band of people on the side of life, sundering themselves from a corrupt society, dates from this time, and it was for "unseen witnesses" that he began to write again. Though in writing *Women in Love* he fought for, and achieved, a new way of seeing destruction as a necessary part of creation, and shed to a moving degree the hysteria and malaise with which he had reacted to the hysteria and malaise that had come upon his world, the novel remains apocalyptic—and it failed to find a publisher until 1920. By that time the Lawrences had left England once more, never to live there again, and had embarked on the series of wanderings which ended only with Lawrence's death in the south of France.

In retrospect, then, *The Rainbow* can be seen to have been both a beginning and an end. It is the last of Lawrence's novels to have been conceived in a prewar world. From the angle of *Women in Love,* it could be imaged as some beautiful landscape (a Beulah, or the Delectable Mountains), reached through private conflict and pilgrimage, but destined to give way to wider and intenser battle, a more final judgment of life and death. Yet *The Rainbow* is also the first revelation of Lawrence's full and strange powers as a novelist. To write it required a searching clarification of his beliefs, a new style, a new kind of characterization. Something was lost from the art of *Sons and Lovers;* far more (I believe) was gained. It was the new dimension of vision, moreover, that enabled Lawrence to achieve his confrontation of a more terrible world in *Women in Love.* It was not the continuation he planned, but it is a sequel nevertheless, and the two novels provide a commentary on each other in which neither need be diminished. The world he wrote about changed, the new vision and art held true, capable of modulation to rise to a sterner challenge. Thereafter, however, his art as a novelist declined, so that *The Rainbow* stands revealed as the foundation of his greatest work. It is also the last of his novels to have been written with a successful novelist's confidence that there exists a public capable of responding to his powers. Though the full effects of his disillusion do not appear immediately, after *The Rainbow* he felt himself increasingly isolated from and antagonistic to the world he had written for, and this was bound to affect the nature of his fiction. He was driven deeper into himself in exploration and discovery, but his art, after *Women in Love,* became more shrill, insistent, and exhortatory. *The Rainbow* is also the last of his novels to take for granted that man develops within a changing society, rather than by sundering himself from it in repudiation. The portrait of society has a scope and complexity in *The Rainbow* that is unique in Lawrence. His social criticism after this becomes more intense and challenging, but narrower, and eventually less convincing.

What is most remarkable about the novel, as the opening chapter makes clear, is its annunciation of a rich tension between social history and universal vision. The first pages present us with the high seriousness of true pastoral, seeking a vantage point from which to see human life in its most basic form, in a timeless world untroubled by historical process or social change. We begin, moreover, not with "characters" or personalities, but with men and women in a universal setting. There is the flat, rich earth, which the eye moves across, binding it into a unified landscape in which man is at one with nature. There is the church tower on the hill, calling the eye up, out, and beyond—what the eighteenth-century artist would have called a "prospect"—a fingerpost pointing to the village, the city, another world of civilization, intellect, and art, the fulfillment of individuality. Between them is the human dwelling, facing both ways. The charged poetic language, rhythmically exploring and opposing the visions of the Men of the Landscape and the Women of the Prospect, reveals the nature of the two opposite impulses that Lawrence detects at work, below the surface of individual personality and conscious motivation, in all men and women everywhere and anytime. Between these two poles, directed by a dialectic of opposite forces, human beings may work out their destinies in different and complex ways; the nature of their conflicts may be affected by the differing personalities of individuals and by the pressures of the particular societies in which they find themselves—yet below and behind, Lawrence clearly believes, the same dialectic will always be discoverable. By isolating, at first, his basic vision from the complication of individual character and social context, Lawrence seeks to clarify the nature of the opposite impulses in themselves. The opening section thus provides a kind of Prelude, a sounding of a pattern of chords which announces the novel's major theme.

The Rainbow differs from *Sons and Lovers* most obviously in this new clarity and universality of vision. Where the Lawrence of the earlier book had to search (sometimes agonizingly) into his own early life to discover its pattern and meaning, the Lawrence of *The Rainbow* confidently opens with the annunciation of a conceptual framework, beautifully realized in imaginative language, and rendered into convincingly human terms of everyday and all time. He had had to work hard for his new insight. We can trace its growth from the unpublished "Preface" to *Sons and Lovers*, through *Twilight in Italy* and the three discarded novels that led up to *The Rainbow*, into the *Study of Thomas Hardy* (where the new "metaphysic" was first really grasped and formulated), and from there into the further embodiment and exploration of *The Rainbow* itself. One of the great leaps forward in the interpretation of the book has come from realization of the importance of the *Study*, though it should not be regarded as a "key," and the novel shows a considerable advance on the more theoretical work.

We are prepared to grasp the dialectic opposition of the forces that the *Study* calls the Law of God the Father, and the Love of God the Son, through their embodiment in the Brangwen Men and Women in the opening pages of the novel. But we shall rapidly discover that we are not meant to think of them as male and female in any simple way, for we shall find both forces operating within individuals of either sex. Nor ought there to be any temptation to choose between them; it seems self-evident from the start that life at either extreme would be life impoverished. The challenge that will face the "characters" who take over from the archetypal Men and Women of the opening, is the challenge to *marry* their oppositions,[1] for, like Blake, Lawrence believed that human progress springs from contraries, and that conflict is creative. We have to use the underlying dialectic imaginatively, in order to understand the complex experience of the three generations of lovers whose relationships Lawrence has set himself to explore. From this angle, the structure of the novel is a comparative one; we look, as it were, at three pictures hung side by side

---

[1] The rainbow or arch (the idea may have come from Forster's "rainbow bridge" in *Howards End*) is of course the one figure which can unite the "horizontal" and "vertical" directions of landscape and prospect.

in a timeless gallery, in order to grasp the nature of their success and limitation by comparison and contrast.

At once however we become aware of complicating perspectives, for the opening chapter is significantly divided into two sections. The first is outside time and character, but as soon as we move into the second, we are confronted by a date, 1840; by an obvious change in the social environment affecting the everyday life of the Brangwens; and by named individuals, no longer Men and Women but this man, that woman. Pastoral fuses with social history. If the major theme remains human relationship seen against a universal perspective, and if the major effort in interpretation has gone into a firmer grasp of that perspective, there is also a vital sense in which Lawrence is concerned with the inner significance for human beings of what happened to England between 1840 and the first years of the twentieth century—and more work needs to be done on this. From this angle, the structure of the novel becomes a progressive series, in which the human potential becomes richer from generation to generation, but the challenge to the marriage of opposites becomes more and more difficult.

Broadly speaking, Lawrence detects three main areas of transformation in English society after 1840. Most obviously there is the industrial revolution, the collieries and factories, the sprawling growth of villages into towns and towns into cities, the advent of suburbia, the coming of canals and railways to serve the new growth, the appearance of the motor car. We watch in the novel a great growth in material prosperity and freedom (but also in ugliness) and an increasing complexity of social organization and social awareness. Even more important for the Lawrence of *The Rainbow*, however, is the great increase in articulateness, knowledge, awareness of the self—the result, of course, of the revolution in education which was perhaps nineteenth-century England's finest achievement. Lawrence himself, the miner's son who could become teacher, poet, novelist, critic, painter, was a phenomenon that could only occur because of what had happened in England, particularly after 1870. And, perhaps most important to him of all, the second half of the nineteenth century had witnessed the decline of religious values; we see very clearly in the novel a steady diminution of significance and meaning in the church, accompanied by the growth of rationalism, of scientific materialism, and of agnostic emancipation. *The Rainbow* is an impressive social document (without overt documentation), and if one were to collect the material it contains under these three headings it would be surprisingly full and extensive.

What seems more important, however, is to establish in broad outline Lawrence's attitude toward these changes. He is, of course, hostile to certain results of the industrial revolution, and is already moving towards his later position as the arch-Dissenter. But we must be careful here. He is not against prosperity, nor is he against the greater scope and freedom that come with it. But his imagination is horrified by the sprawling ugliness which speaks to him of a loss of the sense of organic life and beauty; and even more appalled by the possibility of people losing the sense of their own individuality, and giving or selling themselves to organizations, systems, machines—becoming instrumental. For Lawrence, there is no substitute for individual living, fulfilled in the personal relationships which tap the total personality. Yet the burst canal which drowns Tom Brangwen, and symbolically (as a Flood) marks the ending of an old world, is not a simple disaster. The novel shows very clearly how the increase in freedom and awareness, following after the industrial revolution and growing steadily through the second and third generations, brings an enormous increase in human potential and liberates the life of imagination, art, and intellect. Yet Lawrence has mixed feelings about the second change too, for he clearly focuses the increased difficulty in achieving true relationship that the new dimension of self-awareness brings. In a sentence (of Ursula): "She was aware now. . . . And so, it was more difficult to come to him." Education and emancipation do not bring fulfillment to the new women in the novel; for that can only be found in the marriage of opposites, and awareness of self in Ursula (or Anna) makes it more difficult to abandon the self to the other, the unknown, and fosters the potential destructiveness of self-assertion. In his treatment of formal education, moreover, Lawrence concentrates again on the life-denying effects of system and mechanization. For him, only the free individual can really learn and grow; the only living knowledge is founded in personal and organic life. Once knowledge becomes a commodity, and the organization which purveys it is tied to a world of power, or of materialism and money, it is dead. Lawrence's art seeks to recapture a sense of the mystery of being, like the organic life of the cell under Ursula's microscope. At his greatest he is not the prophet of the Dark Gods; the life of the mind is an essential and forceful pole in the dialectic of *The Rainbow,* but he does set out to right a balance—and he is consequently deeply concerned at the loss of the religious sense. The novel in its deepest aspect is a kind of Bible, recalling its readers to a religious vision of the world. This has nothing to do with religious organizations or creeds; human relationship becomes the only true church. Lawrence rejects Christianity as the religion of death, the denial of the body, a heavenly otherworld. He borrows Christian language and biblical symbols and stories, but he reinterprets or even reverses them—like his treatment of the Noah story—so that death and rebirth, baptism, confirmation, resurrection, occur to individuals through sexual relationship, here and now. Ultimately the rainbow spans the earth with a covenant of infinite possibility for the living; but the vision is only available to the soul newly re-created by abandoning self-direction, and ready to trust itself to the working of divine forces.[2] *The Rainbow* attempts to discover a new prose for God.

The social vision of the novel is a great part of its strength—but we have to allow for a limitation that results from Lawrence's individualism. Behind all his attitudes toward social change lies a central concern with the individual human being as the essential unit of life, and with the relation of individual man and woman as the essential source of creativity. Moreover, the fulfillment they find in the marriage of opposites reveals itself in greater individuation. Though *The Rainbow* is a great study of the effect of changes in society as a whole on the individual being, the vision does seem to lack a middle ground to connect the two. If we compare Lawrence with George Eliot, what has gone is her sense of community, her understanding of how communal relationships intersect with individual relationships. We glimpse a community in change behind the family in *The Rainbow,* but the novel is not concerned to analyze what industrialism and urbanization have done to the old communal relationships of rural England, or the nature of the new forms of community that have taken their place. Consequently, even in *The Rainbow,* the factory, the mine, and the housing estate can be over-simple symbols—the limitation will become more glaring later—and there can be a too easy dichotomy between individual being and collective nonentity. Lawrence's own background may be one explanation of why he never fully shared or truly understood the nature of either working-class or middle-class community; but the limitation is complementary to the strength and intensity of his concern for individual freedom and fulfillment.

His conception of the individual, moreover, was so complex that its full expression demanded a new kind of novel, founded on a new approach to "character." This, of course, is not confined to Lawrence; indeed one might argue[3] that the basic difference between the nineteenth-century and the modern novel lies in a shift from concern

---

[2] These are valid objections to the ending, but these need to be seen in relation to both the nature of Ursula's crisis, and the novel's paradoxical structure. The final vision, like its biblical counterpart, is a conditional covenant, whose cost is clear; and it is not a "conclusion," but (in pointing to the availability in tragedy of divine creativity) a sign that the story is *not* finished.

[3] As Ian Gregor has done in his *The Moral and the Story* (London: Faber & Faber, 1962).

with behavior to a concern with consciousness, of which Lawrence is only part though he carried it further than most. The model for character in nineteenth-century fiction (even, arguably, in George Eliot) is mainly the portrait of man in terms of his actions, which are the outcome of will and choice. We know him by studying his behavior. But in Hardy we can detect a radical shift; he seems far less confident, and sometimes not confident at all, that what his characters do is the important thing. He is interested in what they are, in the signature of their being. We know them most truly not in terms of their behavior but of their consciousness. From this viewpoint, Hardy is perhaps the first modern novelist, though we should detect earlier beginnings in George Eliot. It is Eliot who, for Henry James, "sets a limit to the old-fashioned English novel," but for Lawrence "started it all. It was she who started putting all the action inside."

The shift is completed in *The Rainbow.* The creation of beings whose consciousness is a complex opposition of forces they may only partly understand, perhaps hardly at all, but which operate not only through them but through all the natural universe, required a revolutionary new technique. Moreover Lawrence is increasingly concerned to tap the unconscious; he has his place in the post-Freudian world, though his insights are his own. The art of *Sons and Lovers* combined the dramatic presentation of characters in speech and action, in realistic terms, with a poetic exploration in other scenes of more inward dimensions, in language drawn from nature. But both kinds of scene took place in a sequence of definite time and place; and both explored definite personalities, seen in some new ways, but founded in an older kind of solid specification. Now, however, Lawrence's fiction makes a radical departure. The famous letter to Edward Garnett speaks of the replacement of "the old stable ego" by

> another *ego*, according to whose action the individual is unrecognisable, and passes through, as it were, allotropic states which it needs a deeper sense than any we've been used to exercise, to discover are states of the same single radically unchanged element . . . the characters fall into the form of some other rhythmic form, as when one draws a fiddle-bow across a fine tray delicately sanded, the sand takes lines unknown.

The definite personalities of *Sons and Lovers* give way to more mysterious beings, fluctuating, ever-changing consciousnesses. Lawrence has to discover ways of showing the lines of force which operate on them to make them reveal first one orientation, then another, according to the rhythm of the situation in which they find themselves, while remaining recognizeably the same people (as the Garnett letter insufficiently emphasizes). Scenes regularly acquire rhythmic qualities of change and process which are the essence of their meaning. The style becomes more exploratory, and more poetic not only in its rhythms, but also in a richly suggestive language of image and symbol which we have to see reorchestrated in multiple ways. What Lawrence came to think of as the "hard, violent style" of *Sons and Lovers*, "full of sensation and presentation," gives way to subtler suggestiveness, more tentative processes of exploration. Again, as Roger Sale has argued,[4] the definite time, place, and dramatic situation of *Sons and Lovers* are replaced by a syntax and vocabulary which continually modulate between a specific here and now, and a world beyond time, whose whole space is the inner dimension of being. We have to learn to detect the ways in which insights into the inner dimension of one set of characters are reorchestrated in the exploration of another set, and build up into the progressive organization of the novel as a whole, its patterns of imagery and diction. Yet we have also to see how the vision continually regrounds itself in the concrete presentation of recognizeable people, dramatic situations, and social contexts, in an art of process.

Not surprisingly, *The Rainbow* is much more difficult than *Sons and Lovers*, though it is also (I believe) ultimately far more rewarding. In some ways we are still learning to read it. Many earlier criticisms have been displaced by advances in interpretation: objections to Lawrence's over-insistence have come to seem oddly paired with failures to grasp exactly what is being insisted upon; objections to the irrelevance of some parts of the novel have vanished as we have learned more about its structure; and it has become more difficult to charge that the characters are undifferentiated, as we have grown to understand the nature of Lawrence's analysis. Yet very real critical problems remain. The chief of these has always been the relation between the authorial analysis and the "realized" presentation. There is always a danger in discussing Lawrence of being taken over by him, becoming imprisoned in his language and concepts, and insufficiently critical of how much he shows what he says. There is, I think, equal danger in believing that valid literary criticism can operate without full understanding of a very difficult, complex, and exploratory mind and art. It is not possible, to separate Lawrence the "thinker" or "prophet" (or "bore") from Lawrence the "imaginative artist"—the relationship is organic and indissoluble. Yet in one sense it is true that the new power of systematic analysis that distinguishes *The Rainbow* from *Sons and Lovers* is not an unmixed blessing. The mode of the earlier novel was a curious blend of omniscient author analysis with a more neutral presentation of conflicting views. Lawrence's new analytic power in *The Rainbow* brings with it the danger that the authorial

[4] In "The Narrative Technique of *The Rainbow*," *Modern Fiction Studies* 5 (1959).

voice may become too omniscient and too insistent, that the novelist may put lines into the sand rather than discover them because they are there.[5] Yet the new power demonstrably also called forth an opposing impulse of dramatic and poetic imagination. The new mode of characterization, seeking to break down the old *stable* ego, and substitute a more mysterious, fluid, and tentative vision, and the new style seeking to explore the changing location of conflicting forces within the being, were themselves a check against schematism and authorial certainty. The attempt, in extraordinary leaps of imagination, to penetrate deeper into unconscious movements of the psyche, made Lawrence's art in *The Rainbow* more complex, exploratory, and tentative than before. One of its strengths at its best, is the way that its central emphasis on the creativity of conflict works against our taking sides, or hardening our response or judgment, or neglecting the vital complexities of the fictive human beings. There is criticism of both Anna and Will, Ursula as well as Skrebensky. Nevertheless, as the exploration reaches further outward and inward, and as its metaphoric implications become more extensive, Lawrence's own struggles, to clarify and understand what he has imagined, do involve greater and greater strains on his language. In the finest passages these are triumphantly met, but there is constant danger of pretentiousness, and of nagging repetition, whenever the imagination is less than fully extended. When he failed, however, he failed against his own standards; for perhaps the best criterion for the relation of the art of Being to the art of Understanding remains his own. The final paragraphs of the *Study* argue that the supreme fiction must also be a marriage of opposites, and that it is the tension of opposed impulses that makes both creative. The novelist must create being, that which simply *is,* and to which we respond in togetherness, solidity of sensation and feeling; but he must also create *knowing,* making articulate, differentiating, turning apprehension into comprehension. The life of the novel is to be found in the systole and diastole between these processes, and it is by virtue only of the complementary intensity of both that the novel can hope to see "beyond." His last novel speaks of the "vast importance" of fiction, in that "it can inform and lead into new places the flow of our sympathetic consciousness, and it can lead our sympathy away in recoil from things gone dead. Therefore, the novel, properly handled, can reveal the most secret places of life." *The Rainbow* is not without faults and failures, but it is one of the two novels of Lawrence that can live up to that criterion.

[5] S. L. Goldberg argues a case in *"The Rainbow*: Fiddle-bow and Sand," *Essays in Criticism* 11 (October 1961).

The Originality of *The Rainbow*

by Marvin Mudrick

Manners and morals: they are, critics agree, what novels properly concern themselves with; and the specialist in the English novel can readily demonstrate the English novelist's expert attention to both from *Moll Flanders* to the latest thriller by Graham Greene. Certainly, fiction is of all literary genres the most intractable to description or definition, and we are grateful for any indices to its nature. We are also proud of our language and literature; and the novel in English has an illustrious history, no doubt about it. So the manners and morals, and the fiction we are specially interested in are English and American. It may not, then, seem chauvinistic to us when Caroline Gordon[1] discovers the world history of the novel to be a triumphant progress toward apotheosis in the work of the Anglo-American, Henry James, who was obliging enough to scrutinize, with the tact of an exquisite sensibility, Anglo-Saxon manners and morals—of only a few social groups, to be sure—on *both* sides of the Atlantic. Even Dr. Leavis, who demotes or dismisses Richardson, Fielding, Sterne, Smollett, Dickens, Thackeray, Hardy, and Joyce, expresses much admiration for Hawthorne, and finds a great tradition in Jane Austen, George Eliot, James, Conrad, and Lawrence, in whose work, as it seems to him, manners are so chosen and placed as to reflect on their particular surfaces the image of that sober absolute morality, essentially secular and embattled, which for two centuries has been the strength of England if not of the entire civilized world.

It is just here, regarding the rest of the world, that a doubt arises. Compare, for instance, George Eliot and Tolstoy, or Conrad and Dostoievsky—comparisons that Dr. Leavis, at any rate, ought to accept as fair, since one great tradition ought to be able to stand up

---

"The Originality of The Rainbow*" by Marvin Mudrick. From* Spectrum *3 (Winter 1959): 3–28. Copyright © 1959 by* Spectrum. *Reprinted by permission of the author.*

[1] In *How to Read a Novel,* Viking, 1957.

against another, and since George Eliot and Tolstoy share a preoccupation with the social and ordinary as Conrad and Dostoievsky share a preoccupation with the psychological and extraordinary. Or compare Stendhal and Jane Austen, or Turgenev and James, or almost any nineteenth-century French or Russian novelist and Hawthorne.

Fiction, and a tradition of fiction, may be genuine without being great. Greatness is, after all, relative, and when we compare George Eliot and Tolstoy we are aware of such differences in magnitude that to describe the two of them by the same honorific epithet is to do no service to either. Nor is George Eliot a feeble representative of the tradition Dr. Leavis singles out: *Middlemarch,* at least, is a very impressive novel, with a breadth of intelligent sympathy it fixes for all time the manners and morals of its own place and time, it is perhaps the only English novel that sensitively registers something like a whole society. Yet it is, as the author notes, "A Study of Provincial Life." There is, in fact, no English novel that registers a whole society; and, in the balance with Continental fiction, there is almost no English novel that cannot fairly be described as provincial.

It is not, of course, merely a question of subject: a novelist may be as cosmopolitan as he pleases in treating provincial life—Flaubert or Galdós, for example. The point is that for the English novelist a provincialism of temperament is liable to go along with his provincialism of subject. Mme. Bovary, not to mention Bouvard and Pécuchet, has written some of the better-known English novels, and the sturdy pragmatism of the English petty bourgeoisie has penetrated and sustained English fiction since those redoubtable self-made innovators and moral men of practical affairs, Defoe and Richardson. The English novel has chacteristically been partisan, either protective or rebellious; and the standard of conduct—of manners and morals—which it lavishly illustrates, and by which it measures itself, is the middle-class standard. *Wuthering Heights* and *Tristram Shandy* are as pertinent to the case as *Pamela,* and together they exemplify the three major modes of English fiction: romance as protest, satire as protest, and sentiment as affirmation. Perhaps Dr. Leavis recoils with such a spasm of distaste from Sterne because *Tristram Shandy* is the most subversive protest in English fiction against the bourgeois imperatives that Dr. Leavis, by implication, finds so congenial to the flowering of a great tradition.

These imperatives are, of course, overwhelmingly materialistic. Tom Jones in the hay (sowing his wild oats) with a pretty chambermaid, Scrooge converted to the obsession of giving rather than withholding smiles and crowns and guineas, Pamela indignantly rejecting pre-marital advances for the sake of wealth and rank later—all of them are enjoying the satisfactions of a morality that ultimately, despite its solemn façade, repays its adherents and sinks human problems in cash and Christmas pudding, a morality of trivial appetites. Whether the English novelist is examining, with intelligence or sentimentality or cynicism, the manners and squeamishness of the cultivated provinces, or the local color of urban and rural low life, or the sinister fascinations of the *haut monde,* or the convulsive freakishness of grand super-sexual and asexual passions, or the palpitating idealism of young women who—not having been told what they can importantly do— are looking for something important to do: whatever the English novelist tries, the manners and morals of the earliest and most oppressively successful middle class in history are breathing down his neck and directing his pen into the official view of a life that is in any case considerably less exhilarating than the life visible to the great Continental novelists. Or, for that matter, to Chaucer and Shakespeare.

We must come to it at last, the bourgeois imperative which has defended the materialist order against its gravest threat, and which Anglo-Saxon fiction had perforce to accept for two centuries, the imperative against human normality. You may, the imperative declares, transcend sex by the rhetoric of a grand passion, you may cheapen it as by Fielding's characteristic resort to comic-strip prurience, you may ignore it or jeer at it, you may even in extremity be clinical about it, but you may not regard it as a serious, normal, central preoccupation of mankind, and you may not attempt to understand it.

The first literary effect of such a proscription was to deprive English fiction of normal women. The sphere of decision for women, in Western civilization at least, has always been love and marriage; and if the woman is not permitted to take into account the most serious impulse of her private existence, she may surrender to domesticity or the vapors and become one of Dickens' brave Biddys or dumb Doras, or she may be encouraged to transcend sex before going to the trouble of learning what it is, like George Eliot's Dorothea or Emily Brontë's Cathy or any other Gothic or Romantic heroine. There are even relatively few *interesting* women in English fiction, and most of these are interesting because their authors understand and document the pathology of their reduction: Jane Austen's Emma, Dickens' Estella (his only powerful insight into a woman's sensibility). And there are a very few whose normality has the protective coloration of intelligence and so passes undetected: Jane Austen's Elizabeth Bennet and Anne Elliot, for example. Generally speaking, however, the heroine of English fiction is liable to be a dead loss—think of all the unrememberable Amelias hung like decorative albatrosses round the necks of the heroes of Victorian novels. And then think of Tolstoy's Natasha and Anna, Dostoievsky's women supreme in their passionate abnormality, the whole range of unapologetic women in Stendhal and

Balzac and Flaubert, the gallery of unhurried female sensuality in
Colette: not only a definable *sex* in contrast to the poor sticks of
English heroines, but almost a different species. The English hero,
true, has always been allowed some scope of heroic action in adventure (often commercial), in working his way up, in "becoming a success." Still, to eradicate half the human race, and to confine the energies of the other half mainly within the bounds of materialistic
aspiration—this is not to survey, through morals and manners, the
limits of human possibility. It was this order of things that D. H.
Lawrence confronted when he began writing the novel the first part
of which eventually became *The Rainbow.*

Literary revolutions are as various and frequent as political elec-
tions: some are important, most are not. When what has been called
the Flaubertian tradition (a French import which, though it deeply
influenced two representatives of his own "native" tradition, Dr.
Leavis regards with a somewhat xenophobic distaste) was introduced
into English fiction, and such novelists as James, Conrad, Ford, and
Joyce adopted and developed the techniques available to a conscious
craftsmanship in fiction, one important and irreversible revolution had
occurred—the most important, some critics believe, in the history of
English fiction. Certainly, it produced important and original work,
even though it has inflicted upon us, unavoidably, all the gimmickry
of craft-conscious and myth-mongering and symbolifying criticism,
as well as some of the doleful justification for such criticism in those
pointless manipulations of technique into which the tradition may
tempt the novelist: Conrad, for example, somberly picking his way
through the underbrush of half a dozen intervening points of view, in
that disastrous virtuoso exercise *Chance,* to report on a man's tying a
shoelace.

To this tradition, and to the revolution it achieved, Lawrence does
not belong. Joyce belonged to them, but he participated in another
literary revolution, the revolution against the Anglo-Saxon (and Irish)
censor; and here he and Lawrence may be said to have stood in a
common cause. Joyce's publishing and distributing difficulties with
Dubliners and *Ulysses* strikingly resemble Lawrence's with *The Rainbow* and *Lady Chatterley's Lover.* Nevertheless, there is censorship
and censorship. When Judge Woolsey issued his celebrated decision
admitting *Ulysses* into the United States, he remarked, in denying
that it came within the legal definition of obscenity, that its effect on
the reader was more likely to be "emetic" than "aphrodisiac." The
interesting judicial principle was thus established that, for the Anglo-
Saxon commonwealth, to vomit is, if not positively healthier, at least
less baneful than to engage in sexual intercourse. The judge rightly
inferred that Joyce's sexual imagery and naughty language were no

vital threat at all to Anglo-Saxon mores, but only the signs by which
a whole culture manifested its nausea and self-disgust. The Joycean
Revolution of the Word has brought freedom, it is now obvious,
mainly for cynical clinicians and cautious pornographers, the freedom
to spit and hiss (and leads directly to such a May-fly oddity of literary
entomology as the San Francisco Renaissance). Today, a quarter-cen-
tury after the canonization of Molly Bloom, the Woolseyan principle
has been challenged: *Lady Chatterley's Lover,* which audaciously attempted to rehabilitate sexual imagery and the old Anglo-Saxon words
as signs of health and tenderness (and which, by the way, succeeded),
has at last been legally published in both the United States and the
United Kingdom.

Still, *Lady Chatterley's Lover* is, by the pressures of its subject
and of the lateness of its hour, as close to being hortatory as a work
of art can afford to be; even without its four famous words (all of
them used more frequently, of course, in *Ulysses* and in almost any
current popular novel), its radical extra-literary intent is clear. *The
Rainbow*—which marked the outbreak of the Lawrencian revolution
—is in fact a more dangerous work because it is less open to philistine
retaliation, because it bases itself confidently on no exhortation at all,
only on the assumption that sex is a serious, normal, central preoccupation of mankind. After its early skirmish with suppression (which
showed, not how acutely prescient, but how very silly, English censors
could be in 1915), *The Rainbow* has been widely accessible in print,
and is even becoming generally accepted—at least the first half of it
—as a brilliant record of English manners and morals over three generations, a *really* great English family-chronicle novel, not less respectable and beyond comparison better than anything in this line by
Arnold Bennett.

True enough, there is, beside it, no family-chronicle novel in English that deserves mention; and anything that will certify the re-
spectability of *The Rainbow* is to be prized, just as we ought to prize
Lawrence's subliterary reputation as a sensational novelist for making
more of his fiction accessible in cheap-paperback American reprints
than that of any other major English author. *The Rainbow* is not,
after all, so respectable as Galsworthy: there are reasons for Lawrence's
notoriety, as well as for his boring and disappointing the common
reader to whom he is notorious; and the reasons are all in *The Rainbow.* Nothing promises to be more, and proves on inspection to be
less, sensational than this family-chronicle novel which assumes not
only that generations are generated, but that the relationship between
husband and wife is the central fact of human existence, that the living nucleus of this relationship is the act of sexual union, that the act
of sexual union is infinitely serious, complex, and difficult, and that an

act of such radiant significance must be fairly treated by the honest novelist.

Graham Hough, however, disapproves of Lawrence's candor: "As for physical passion . . . no one should try to present it as . . . [Lawrence] does, and traditional literary good sense has always known it." [2] This appeal to timeless good taste would be plausible, if it were not for the very special conditions against which Lawrence had to contend. Most authors of the past, and of other cultures, who have dealt with physical passion have not, indeed, presented it directly. Chaucer did not, nor did Colette; but the reason is that neither needs to: for Chaucer, the sacramental nature of passion and, for Colette, the various joys of an indulged sensuality are self-evident and unchallenged; medieval Catholic humanism and modern French hedonism meet in their conviction of the power of sexual gratification, which can bring to peace and stillness men and women alike. Lawrence, very much on the other hand, has a unique problem: he must reassert this life-renewing power against two centuries of a culture and literature that have muffled and denied its very existence, and he can reassert it only by presenting its actuality as a reminder to the deaf and blind. Lawrence's terrible candor is necessary only because there has been so mendacious and destructive a silence; and yet, because it is so peremptorily called for, it not only reclaims old truths but rushes on to make discoveries. The long reign of English philistinism—in both life and letters—is Lawrence's provocation and his unexampled opportunity.

Of course Lawrence has the advantage of springing from the country community of English workingmen-farmers, a community not bound or even much influenced by the shopkeeper code, and he comes to maturity at a time when the whole structure of class and community is about to encounter the disintegrating shock of the First World War. In his historic moment, Lawrence has before him the life of the last English community: not the manners of the province (which are in any case the manners of the provincial petty bourgeoisie and minor gentry), but a life rich in productive labor and in continuity with the passing seasons, rooted in the earthly and physical, inarticulate without grossness or stupidity, a life seemingly permanent yet fated to pass away in the general breakdown of codes and communities and to be replaced or transcended—if by anything—by individual aspiration. It is this process, over three generations, which is the subject and theme of *The Rainbow*; the process is the most momentous human fact of the past century; and it is a process which, in *The Rainbow*, discloses itself poignantly and most crucially in the sexual

[2] In *The Dark Sun*, Duckworth (London), 1956, p. 63.

histories of individuals. The revolutionary nature of *The Rainbow* is, then, twofold: it is the first English novel to record the normality and significance of physical passion; and it is the only English novel to record, with a prophetic awareness of consequences, the social revolution whereby Western man lost his sense of community and men— more especially, women—learned, if they could, that there is no help any longer except in the individual and in his capacity for a passional life.

As soon as the critic of Lawrence begins to favor such terms as "community" and "passion," he risks being suspected of imagining, obsequiously on cue from his author, a unanimity of social feeling that never was and a potency of personal feeling that never could be, under idyllic and perpetually recurring circumstances in the rural districts of the English Midlands up to, say, the turn of our century. But Lawrence presents no idylls. The community in *The Rainbow*, like every other, is an abstraction from its individuals, who are its only embodiment; and it lives as more than a mere term of discourse only so long as it provides forms and sanctions for the abiding impulses of their separate natures. These impulses are, besides, not all of them communal and sympathetic: Lawrence's individuals are just that, different and distinct from one another except when a strength of sympathy draws them together for moments out of the reciprocal alienations of individuality; and every relationship in *The Rainbow* testifies, not how easy and renewable, but how hard to come by, how precarious, and how irrecoverably unique each instance of passion is, even in a nature as faithful to itself and as sensitively patient as Tom Brangwen's:

Then she said:
"You will be good to me, won't you?"
She was small and girlish and terrible, with a queer, wide look in her eyes. His heart leaped in him, in anguish of love and desire, he went blindly to her and took her in his arms.
"I want to," he said as he drew her closer and closer in. She was soothed by the stress of his embrace, and remained quite still, relaxed against him, mingling in to him. And he let himself go from past and future, was reduced to the moment with her. In which he took her and was with her and there was nothing beyond, they were together in an elemental embrace beyond their superficial foreignness. But in the morning he was uneasy again. She was still foreign and unknown to him. Only, within the fear was pride, belief in himself as mate for her. And she, everything forgotten in her new hour of coming to life, radiated vigour and joy, so that he quivered to touch her.
It made a great difference to him, marriage. Things became remote and of so little significance, as he knew the powerful source of his life,

eyes opened on a new universe, and he wondered in thinking of his
triviality before. A new, calm relationship showed to him in the things
he saw, in the cattle he used, the young wheat as it eddied in a wind.

And each time he returned home, he went steadily, expectantly, like
a man who goes to a profound, unknown satisfaction. At dinnertime,
he appeared in the doorway, hanging back a moment from entering, to
see if she was there. He saw her setting the plates on the white-
scrubbed table. Her arms were slim, she had a slim body and full skirts,
she had a dark, shapely head with close-banded hair. Somehow it was
her head, so shapely and poignant, that revealed her his woman to him.
As she moved about clothed closely, full-skirted and wearing her little
silk apron, her dark hair smoothly parted, her head revealed itself to
him in all its subtle, intrinsic beauty, and he knew she was his woman,
he knew her essence, that it was his to possess. And he seemed to live
thus in contact with her, in contact with the unknown, the unaccount-
able and incalculable.

They did not take much notice of each other, consciously.

"I'm betimes," he said.

"Yes," she answered.

He turned to the dogs, or to the child if she were there. The little
Anna played about the farm, flitting constantly in to call something to
her mother, to fling her arms round her mother's skirts, to be noticed,
perhaps caressed, then, forgetting, to slip out again.

Then Brangwen, talking to the child, or to the dog between his knees,
would be aware of his wife, as, in her tight, dark bodice and her lace
fichu, she was reaching up to the corner cupboard. He realized that he
lived by her. Did he own her? Was she here for ever? Or might she go
away? She was not really his, it was not a real marriage, this marriage
between them. She might go away. He did not feel like a master, husband, father of her children. She belonged elsewhere. Any moment, she
might be gone. And he was ever drawn to her, drawn after her, with
ever-raging, ever-unsatisfied desire. He must always turn home, wherever
his steps were taking him, always to her, and he could never quite
reach her, he could never quite be satisfied, never be at peace, because
she might go away.

At evening, he was glad. Then, when he had finished in the yard,
and come in and washed himself, when the child was put to bed, he
could sit on the other side of the fire with his beer on the hob and his
long white pipe in his fingers, conscious of her there opposite him, as
she worked at her embroidery, or as she talked to him, and he was safe
with her now, till morning. She was curiously self-sufficient and did not
say very much. Occasionally she lifted her head, her grey eyes shining
with a strange light, that had nothing to do with him or with this place,
and would tell him about herself. She seemed to be back again in the
past, chiefly in her childhood or her girlhood, with her father. She very
rarely talked of her first husband. But sometimes, all shining-eyed, she
was back at her own home, telling him about the riotous times, the trip

to Paris with her father, tales of the mad acts of the peasants when a burst of religious, self-hurting fervour had passed over the country.

Tom Brangwen's apprehensions are not, after all, merely the customary timeless ones of husbands, but unprecedented seismic shocks: *The Rainbow* is recording a community in its last flare of vitality and gradual dying away, and all relationships and feelings are shaken by the great change. The foreignness of Tom's wife represents, disturbingly enough, the essential distance between all men and especially between the sexes; but it is already a terrifying difference beyond natural difference. Tom is no simple farmer: his aspiration toward the irreducibly alien woman is an inarticulate but not unconscious aspiration toward the experience of a life beyond the receding satisfactions of a community in process of dissolution. Till he meets Lydia he refuses, in drink and solitude, the only life his community offers him. Now, his dissatisfactions are new, and the brave chances he takes are new.

It was the coming of the colliery, years before, bringing canal and railway through the Brangwen land, which cut across the past and offered a promise of the future:

> As they drove home from town, the farmers of the land met the blackened colliers trooping from the pit-mouth. As they gathered the harvest, the west wind brought a faint, sulphurous smell of pit-refuse burning. As they pulled the turnips in November, the sharp clink-clink-clink-clink-clink of empty trucks shunting on the line, vibrated in their hearts with the fact of other activity going on beyond them.

Tom, the young farmer awakened to a troubled sense of the restrictions of the Brangwen life, comes eventually into his own vision of a life beyond, once he has had his encounter with the complaisant pretty girl and his little talk with her Frenchman escort, the "ageless" and "monkey-like," gracious and imperial gentleman from elsewhere. When Tom sees the foreign lady walking toward him on the road, he knows that she is the awful chance he must take, and the best he can do. Yet the impulse outward moves, necessarily, more rapidly than the possibility of comprehending and fulfilling it: the breakup of the community is too sudden and unanticipated as railways and canals cut across the enclosed spaces of the mind, and the individual is freed from traditional unquestioned preoccupations in order to think and do—what? Tom Brangwen seeks out and lives with strangeness; but his satisfaction and his anguish remain equally resistant to statement or analysis, shy of words, still therefore plausibly connected with the old inarticulate traditional world. His steadiness, halfway between two worlds, is constantly in danger from the incompleteness of its commitment to either; it can be shaken, as by his stepdaughter, Anna, whom he desperately loves but who has come too far from the past to rest in mute suspensions of judgment:

> She tried to discuss people, she wanted to know what was meant. But her father became uneasy. He did not want to have things dragged into consciousness. Only out of consideration for her he listened. And there was a kind of bristling rousedness in the room. The cat got up and stretching itself, went uneasily to the door. Mrs. Brangwen was silent, she seemed ominous. Anna could not go on with her fault-finding, her criticism, her expression of dissatisfactions. She felt even her father against her.

Individual aspiration, once it is released, has no certain or obvious goal; and how can it be held in check somewhere, how can one keep it from making all action or repose seem premature and insufficient, how can the skeptical analytic mind be quieted? In fact, even for Tom these questions have force, the speechless remoteness of his marriage—for all of its passion—is finally not enough, his pathetic paternal jealousy of his stepdaughter's choice of a husband poisons even as it recalls to him his sense of his own life:

> What was missing in his life, that, in his ravening soul, he was not satisfied? He had had that friend at school, his mother, his wife, and Anna? What had he done? He had failed with his friend, he had been a poor son; but he had known satisfaction with his wife, let it be enough; he loathed himself for the state he was in over Anna. Yet he was *not* satisfied. It was agony to know it.
>
> Was his life nothing? Had he nothing to show, no work? He did not count his work, anybody could have done it. What had he known, but the long, marital embrace with his wife! Curious, that this was what his life amounted to! At any rate, it was something, it was eternal. He would say so to anybody, and be proud of it. He lay with his wife in his arms, and she was still his fulfillment, just the same as ever. And that was the be-all and the end-all. Yes, and he was proud of it.
>
> But the bitterness, underneath, that there still remained an unsatisfied Tom Brangwen, who suffered agony because a girl cared nothing for him. He loved his sons—he had them also. But it was the further, the creative life with the girl, he wanted as well. Oh, and he was ashamed. He trampled himself to extinguish himself.

So Tom Brangwen dies, drunk as Noah to forget the wearying puzzles of his middle age, drowned in the flood of rain, and his women mourn him:

> They cleared and washed the body, and laid it on the bed.
>
> There, it looked still and grand. He was perfectly calm in death, and, now he was laid in line, inviolable, unapproachable. To Anna, he was

the majesty of the inaccessible male, the majesty of death. It made her still and awe-stricken, almost glad.

Lydia Brangwen, the mother, also came and saw the impressive, inviolable body of the dead man. She went pale, seeing death. He was beyond change or knowledge, absolute, laid in line with the infinite. What had she to do with him? He was a majestic Abstraction, made visible now for a moment, inviolate, absolute. And who could lay claim to him, who could speak of him, of the him who was revealed in the stripped moment of transit from life into death? Neither the living nor the dead could claim him, he was both the one and the other, inviolable, inaccessibly himself.

"I shared life with you, I belong in my own way to eternity," said Lydia Brangwen, her heart cold, knowing her own singleness.

"I did not know you in life. You are beyond me, supreme now in death," said Anna Brangwen, awe-stricken, almost glad.

This is Everyman, not at all the conventional individualist hero of English fiction; and Lawrence, anticipating perplexity, provided his critics with a long peg on which to hang their theories about *The Rainbow* and *Women in Love*. "You mustn't look," he wrote to Edward Garnett, who had been disappointed to find no trace of *Sons and Lovers* in the new work, ". . . for the old stable *ego* of the character. There is another ego, according to whose action the individual is unrecognizable, and passes through, as it were, allotropic states which it needs a deeper sense than any other we've been used to exercise, to discover are states of the same single radically unchanged element." And he goes on to make obligingly explicit the analogy of diamond-carbon to the mode of characterization he has just begun to feel at home in. Now this tip from the essentially kindly Lawrence to his bewildered English friend is a useful one; for the elucidation of *Women in Love* especially, as Mark Schorer has pointed out.[3] It is nevertheless not so simple, or perhaps even so accurate, as it looks; and it does not indicate anything nearly so unprecedented— if one takes into account Continental fiction—as Lawrence appears to think.

The trouble is that, in this formulation, Lawrence does not yet seem to have made clear to himself why the old mode of characterization is being discarded and how the new mode functions, and what sort of novel employs one or the other. *Sons and Lovers* is—like *A Portrait of the Artist as a Young Man*—a wilful and confused post-Victorian novel of youthful longing and self-discovery, written by a young man whose *parti pris* rejects or ignores the values of the community which has helped to make him; *The Rainbow,* on the other

[3] *"Women in Love"* in *The Achievement of D. H. Lawrence,* ed. Frederick J. Hoffman and Harry T. Moore, 1953, pp. 163–177.

hand, is an elegiac novel about the dissolution of a community whose values, even as these pass away, the author neither rejects nor ignores but seeks to understand and somehow, for his characters' sake, to transcend. The characters (Mr. Morel excepted) in *Sons and Lovers* are post-Victorian individualists colliding with an angry young individualist of a hero; the characters in *The Rainbow* breathe and move, as long as they can, in the large atmosphere of a community. Not that Tom Brangwen is less *individual* than, say, Paul Morel; quite the contrary, he is more honestly and totally imagined, and therefore more human and more of a man. If the novelist creates his characters as more or less aggressive bundles of recognizable traits, as egos stabilized by manners and morals, and his novel as a sequence of collisions between such bundles, he will produce the kind of novel that Lawrence is now giving up, the novel preoccupied—whether in affirmation or in protest—with manners and morals, the class novel, the standard English novel. If, however, the novelist creates his characters in a life-size medium, fictional and communal, which nurtures, provokes, and makes room for the strength of impulse, he will produce a novel like *The Rainbow*—or *Anna Karenina,* or *The Idiot,* or *The Red and the Black.* Characters in novels like these are not caricatures or even conventional heroes, mere victims or arbiters of manners and morals, they are passions and first principles; and they are all the more human and individual for being so. Nor, of course, is Lawrence's new mode of characterization unprecedented or revolutionary, it is only not very English.

What *is* revolutionary in *The Rainbow*—what makes Lawrence, in perhaps the most important sense, the only modern novelist—is not the mode of characterization, but the new awareness which finds this mode necessary: the awareness that with the dying away, in the age of technology, of genuine communal relations between men, with the inevitable thwarting of what Lawrence was later to call "the societal impulse," the only hope for man lies in those remaining potentialities of human relationships which depend for their realization on the fullest (not necessarily the most various or complicated) possible realization of the sexual impulse. Lawrence, being English, had in this respect no choice but to be revolutionary. English novelists, as spokesmen for the most advanced middle class in the world, had since Defoe been advocating the simplest escape from the intolerable human problems posed by industrialism—the escape into materialist success, the pursuit of what Dickens' Wemmick poignantly euphemizes under the phrase "portable property"; but with the end of the expansive romantic phase of English industrialism, no serious English writer could any longer believe in this escape and pursuit, as Dickens and others before and after could believe in it once it had been sweetened by contrition, materialist benevolence, and marital union with another form of portable property. (We cannot imagine a French or an Italian or a Russian Lawrence, just as we cannot imagine an English Dostoievsky, though the awareness of which Lawrence is both creator and instrument has, finally, as much to say to the Continent as Dostoievsky has to say to the English.) For Lawrence, then, the hope, in fact the last resort, of modern man is—the unhappy word stares at us as it did at Lawrence's censors—sex: not as cold appetite, not as self-imposed exile from the teeming world, not as the exploiting of sensation or the temporary allaying of an itch, but as the bond of tranquillity and faith between man and woman, those polar opponents, and the last removable proof of human community.

The Rainbow is midpassage and arrival. Tom Brangwen still has roots, connections, the virtue of quietness in solitude; of these vestiges of community Anna and Will still keep something by, as it were, barely remembering them, Anna in her slovenly cheerful maternity, Will in his mute satisfaction with manual labor or minor artisanship. Only Ursula—modern woman and therefore, in her unforeseen and disastrously unprepared-for homelessness, true representative of modern mankind—has nothing at all of what, outside themselves, sustained the two generations before her. And for all three generations the unmapped territory to be explored, with increasing desperation and hope, is sex.

Tom Brangwen has a real marriage, notwithstanding its ultimate vulnerability to the stress of uncomprehended change; his apparently unwarrantable youthful waiting for a strangeness beyond his ordinary experience is rewarded and vindicated, and his life is transfigured by the reality of passion. If his marriage fails to give him everything, it nevertheless gives him much, even enough to make him at length unhappily sensitive to the unknown vibrations of what he must do without.

For Anna and Will, on the other hand, marriage seems at first sunnier and more simple. They have moved very far out of the shadow of the old Brangwen world; Anna, at least, is impatient with established sanctities; and both of them rejoice on their prolonged honeymoon in an uninhibited mutual exploration of sexuality, day after day of vital time-dissolving ease:

> As they lay close together, complete and beyond the touch of time or change, it was as if they were at the very centre of all the slow wheeling of space and the rapid agitation of life, deep, deep inside them all, at the centre where there is utter radiance, and eternal being, and the silence absorbed in praise: the steady core of all movements, the unawakened sleep of all wakefulness. They found themselves there, and they lay still, in each other's arms; for their moment they were at the

heart of eternity, whilst time roared far off, forever far off, towards the rim.

Then gradually they were passed away from the supreme centre, down the circles of praise and joy and gladness, further and further out, towards the noise and the friction. But their hearts had burned and were tempered by the inner reality, they were unalterably glad.

Gradually they began to wake up, the noises outside became more real. They understood and answered the call outside. They counted the strokes of the bell. And when they counted midday, they understood that it was midday, in the world, and for themselves also.

It dawned upon her that she was hungry. She had been getting hungrier for a lifetime. But even yet it was not sufficiently real to rouse her. A long way off she could hear the words, "I am dying of hunger." Yet she lay still, separate, at peace, and the words were unuttered. There was still another lapse.

And then, quite calmly, even a little surprised, she was in the present, and was saying:

"I am dying with hunger."

"So am I," he said calmly, as if it were of not the slightest significance. And they relapsed into the warm, golden stillness. And the minutes flowed unheeded past the window outside.

Then suddenly she stirred against him.

"My dear, I am dying of hunger," she said.

It was a slight pain to him to be brought to.

"We'll get up," he said, unmoving.

And she sank her head on to him again, and they lay still, lapsing. Half consciously, he heard the clock chime the hour. She did not hear.

"Do get up," she murmured at length, "and give me something to eat."

"Yes," he said, and he put his arms round her, and she lay with her face on him. They were faintly astonished that they did not move. The minutes rustled louder at the window.

"Let me go then," he said.

She lifted her head from him, relinquishingly. With a little breaking away, he moved out of bed, and was taking his clothes. She stretched out her hand to him.

"You are so nice," she said, and he went back for a moment or two.

Then actually he did slip into some clothes, and, looking round quickly at her, was gone out of the room. She lay translated again into a pale, clearer peace. As if she were a spirit, she listened to the noise of him downstairs, as if she were no longer of the material world.

In such moments as Lawrence here presents, there can be no "characters" in the conventional fictional sense: the mode of characterization is dictated by the focus of attention, which here is on a core of impulse anterior to personality. It is, of course, easy to misunderstand such a passage in the context of English fiction, especially that sort of woman's fiction of which *Jane Eyre* is a quasi-serious instance: the emotion of romantic love reduces heroine (or hero) to a fluttering impotency—especially in anticipation—that may resemble a reduction to impulse. But the conjugal satisfactions of Tom Brangwen, or Anna, or Will, are not reductive at all, they liberate universal human powers, far from making romantic victims they make those relations between people without which there are only egos in collision and no persons. Nobody, it is true, can live indefinitely at such a depth of impulse; and the comic ascension of Anna and Will to the level of a more mundane appetite testifies not only to the existence of a daylight world in which we are all, more or less, scrupulously differentiated fictional characters, but also to that respect for full human truth which disciplines even the most rhapsodic utterances in this novel. The careful reader never forgets that *The Rainbow* is, in one large and traditional aspect, a great realistic novel: Tom Brangwen's life outside marriage, for example, is registered with an immediacy and resonance that would establish him as one of the great figures in English fiction even if he were nothing more; and one thinks of such superb set-pieces as Tom's efforts at comforting the child Anna while Lydia is bearing his first child, Tom's drunkenly inspired eulogy of marriage, his death in the flood—a luminous pertinence of detail, a fidelity to locale, a sternness of pathos not readily matched in any other fiction. Nevertheless, as the rhythm of the style—always near, when not actually, the rhythm of rhapsodic utterance—persists in implying, life is renewable only and perpetually at the springs of impulse, in celebration and praise, where we are less unique than human; and only to the degree to which we have renewed ourselves there, can we breathe and move as individuals in the daylight world.

Renewal, the gift and aim of life, becomes in modern marriage less and less the gift of repose, more and more pressingly the aim of conscious and personal exploration: woman is less passive and man more anxious, approaching an uneasy identity of roles. Lydia is still withdrawn and enigmatic, a woman of the old dispensation, unharried, immured in domesticity and unamenable to self-questioning; so Tom is the explorer—joyous or baffled—in this first marriage, moving doubtfully at the rim of awareness. Anna, on the other hand, has come awake, because the invasion of all things by mechanism and the conscious mind has made Lydia the last possible woman of her kind: having lost what her mother unquestionably had, Anna must make up for it by becoming explorative in her own right, the free companion of her husband. But, after the shared bliss of the honeymoon, the difficulties of the new dispensation become gradually manifest. When the communal sanction for marriage is dissipated and only free and equal individuals remain, the burden on accidents of personality grows suddenly enormous. The temperamental differences between Lydia and

Tom were unbridgeable, and of no significance to Lydia. Yet Will's
soft inarticulateness drives the skeptical articulate Anna wild, and
Anna's attacks on her husband's temperament drive him into retalia-
tory fury:

> She . . . clung to the worship of human knowledge. Man must die
> in the body but in his knowledge he was immortal. Such, somewhere,
> was her belief, quite obscure and unformulated. She believed in the
> omnipotence of the human mind.
>
> He, on the other hand, blind as a subterranean thing, just ignored the
> human mind and ran after his own dark-souled desires, following his
> own tunnelling nose. She felt often she must suffocate. And she fought
> him off.
>
> Then he, knowing he was blind, fought madly back again, frantic in
> sensual fear. He did foolish things. He asserted himself on his rights, he
> arrogated the old position of master of the house.
>
> "You've a right to do as I want," he cried.
>
> "Fool!" she answered. "Fool!"
>
> "I'll let you know who's master," he cried.
>
> "Fool!" she answered. "Fool! I've known my own father, who could
> put a dozen of you in his pipe and push them down with his finger-end.
> Don't I know what a fool you are!"

In the perilous colloidal tension of modern marriage, too much
depends on merely personal qualities. And—at least for persons living
in the delusive afterglow of the old world, still unalert to the swarm-
ing problems of consciousness—too much depends on the increasingly
elaborate and conscious satisfactions of sexuality: the man, having
lost his inherited mastery, comes to depend on these as on a drug, and
the woman comes to resent what she will eventually regard as his
infantile male weakness. Variety, the avoidance of monotony, becomes
more and more a brutal conjugal compulsion. At length, reciprocally
excited by Will's brush with infidelity, Anna and Will give themselves
to the pleasures of a sort of democratic sexual cannibalism, to the
fetishistic daylight fevers of sensuality, the manipulation of bodies as
instruments for pleasure; and if Lawrence's imagery in this passage
plainly obliges us to find the experience analogous to the Fall, it
obliges us also to see the new experiences as a necessary expansion of
man's knowledge in the time of another forced departure from the
garden. Still, Anna and Will never reclaim their honeymoon fulfillment of passion or seem capable of the reconciliation between passion
and sensuality; and their lives dwindle away in subtle disorganization,
in the minor consummations and complaints of Anna's role as the
fecund housewife and Will's as a woodwork teacher for the town,
"very happy and keen in his new public spirit." Since their imperfect
truce is the first modern marriage, it is appropriate that they bring

into being the first complete modern woman, totally dispossessed and therefore totally explorative.

The child Ursula still has her father's environing and sometimes overpowering love; and she has, also in conversation with her grandmother, a window on the certainties of the past even as the thought of growing up without such certainties begins to trouble her:

> . . . Ursula asked her deepest childish questions of her grandmother.
> "Will somebody love me, grandmother?"
> "Many people love you, child. We all love you."
> "But when I am grown up, will somebody love me?"
> "Yes, some man will love you, child, because it's your nature. And I hope it will be somebody who will love you for what you are, and not for what he wants of you. But we have a right to want what we want."
> Ursula was frightened, hearing these things. Her heart sank, she felt she had no ground under her feet. She clung to her grandmother. Here was peace and security. Here, from her grandmother's peaceful room, the door opened on to the greater space, the past, which was so big, that all it contained seemed tiny; loves and births and deaths, tiny units and features within a vast horizon. That was great relief, to know the tiny importance of the individual, within the great past.

Lydia's wisdom in old age is wasted on her granddaughter, and reverberates outward into the large implications of the novel. One of the dangers of marriage in the time of a breaking of bonds is, as Lydia suggests, that a man may be driven to seek in a mate not a distinct and different person as generous and needy as himself, but only what will compensate him, somehow, for his sense of loss—though, tragically, he must have both in order to have either. The marriage of Anna and Will is, at last, a deadlock because neither wife nor husband has the generosity and wisdom to acknowledge and accept the unbreakable differentness of the other; and Tom's response to Lydia's strangeness—at the beginning so compelling an attraction for him—is, at last, to drift back into confusion and the oblivion of drink. Moreover, the grandmother's words to the child Ursula are a prophecy; for Skrebensky will desperately seek in Ursula (as Will sought in Anna) only what might make up for his unmanning sense of loss, and Ursula herself will not understand, not at least till very late, that her promiscuity with Skrebensky is no generous gift of love but only a confession of mutual weakness, no passionate resolution but an increasingly unsatisfactory escape into sex from the unprecedented problems of the modern consciousness.

In the new world there are no landmarks or guideposts, the great past is no longer even a memory, everyone is free and dispossessed; so Ursula's life becomes, necessarily enough, a kind of adventure in limbo. Yet it is this concluding section—in bulk, more than half—of the novel that has been most vexatious and unrewarding for readers; and any effort to assess *The Rainbow* bumps hard against it. No doubt, the section is less satisfying than most of what has come before: it is unduly repetitive, it is occasionally content to make points by assertion rather than by incident, it sometimes mistakes mere detailed documentation for thematic illustration and development, its tone sometimes verges on stridency. There are, after all, too many and too similar descriptions of Ursula and Skrebensky making hopeless love; the career of Ursula as a teacher, however interesting it may be in its own right, is recorded at too much length and with too little relevance to the theme of the novel; and when Lawrence, in his haste to dismiss dry book-learning, tries to palm off on us so trivially literary a truism about college life as this—

> College was barren, cheap, a temple converted to the most vulgar, petty commerce. Had she not gone to hear the echo of learning pulsing back to the source of the mystery?—The source of mystery! And barrenly, the professors in their gowns offered commercial commodity that could be turned to good account in the examination-room; ready-made stuff too, and not really worth the money it was intended to fetch; which they all knew.

—when Lawrence settles for this sort of thing, we are persuaded that he is no longer, for the time being at any rate, attending to the seriousness of his theme. It is perhaps more to the point to agree with Dr. Leavis that Lawrence, his mind already on the very different second novel which had detached itself from this original conception of a single novel on marriage, was trying to finish *The Rainbow* with less sympathy than conscientiousness: in this view, the frustrating account of Ursula's long and strenuous career of frustration may be taken as the result of Lawrence's prudent desire to save her consummation for *Women in Love*.

Still, *The Rainbow* is, finally, not about consummation but about promise. The rainbow that Ursula sees at the very end of the novel need not be dismissed as a despairing symbolic stroke to allow a nominal conclusion and to release Lawrence for *Women in Love*; though the two novels are obviously related in ways more important than the continuance of several characters through the second, it may be that those readers who find the end of *The Rainbow* wanting have turned their minds prematurely to the next book, and are expecting what it is not in the theme of the earlier novel to give. No doubt Lawrence's original intention was to write a single novel which would encompass and illustrate in the lives of a family the great social and psychological change of our century, and which would conclude with a treatment of such individual problems and individual solutions as, indeed, are treated in *Women in Love*. But it must have become eventually clear to him that the breakdown of community was a subject in itself, and that it culminated appropriately in the coming to consciousness of emancipated, modern woman. If Lawrence had ended the novel with modern woman numbed in her grimace of freedom, he would have been merely cynical; if he had ended with Ursula still unsure of her feelings for Skrebensky, the novel would trail off in a puzzle. The novel does, in fact, end as Ursula, having freed herself of her struggle with Skrebensky, is for the first time genuinely free not only of the unrevivable past but of those false ties she has tentatively accepted in place of it. To require any more—at least schematically—is to require an unequivocal happy ending, and even in *Women in Love* or *Lady Chatterley's Lover* Lawrence is not so obliging as that.

The fault is, then, not of scheme but of execution: much of the last half of *The Rainbow* seems to have been written with a slackening of Lawrence's attention to proportion and detail. Yet much is finely done. Something as difficult, for instance, as the relationship between Ursula and Miss Inger comes off without damage to our sympathy for Ursula, and with strong pertinence to the theme. In a time when the injunctions of community and family have been broken, when the in-dividual is responsible only to himself and to his own impulses, why should not Ursula first admire and then fiercely love the handsome, independent woman who so resembles what she herself wishes to be? And why should the warmth and physical responsiveness of her feel-ings be curbed? No mere prohibition will do, for sanctions and pro-hibitions alike have gone under. It is only by living through the ex-perience that Ursula can judge its sinister misleadingness for her: to be free like Winifred Inger is to take pleasure only in the thrill of physiological or mechanical process, to handle and reject, to give noth-ing, to hate one's humanness and to deny the possibility of relation-ship—as Ursula discovers during the visits to her uncle's colliery:

> His real mistress was the machine, and the real mistress of Winifred was the machine. She too, Winifred, worshipped the impure abstrac-tion, the mechanisms of matter. There, there, in the machine, in service of the machine, was she free from the clog and degradation of human feeling. There, in the monstrous mechanism that held all matter, living or dead, in its service, did she achieve her consummation and her per-fect unison, her immortality.

The narcissistic delights of homosexuality are not enough, even for Winifred Inger; even she must make a commitment to something out-side herself, and she finds her consummation and her unison, her im-mortality, in the machine. But Ursula continues to seek hers in the

flesh. Perhaps the repetitive savageries of Ursula's sexual encounters
with Skrebensky are partly justifiable on the ground that with Skrebensky Ursula's attempt is so much more plausible and at the same
time so much more exacerbating: at least Skrebensky is a man and no
narcissistic projection of herself, though she can master and break
him; at least Skrebensky is not positively evil, though he is weak and
inchoate. If we do not lose sympathy with Ursula for her annihilating
cruelty toward Skrebensky, it is because we are convinced that she
suffers in the grip of an impulse which is, if it can ever be fulfilled,
the sanest and most healing impulse accessible to her; if she appears
at moments in the guise of a female spider devouring her sexually
spent and useless mate, she is in any case obeying a brute instinct
more vital than Skrebensky's attachment to political abstractions or
Miss Inger's attachment to mechanism. Ursula's quest is desperate, so
therefore are her feelings often; but the discoveries she must make
cannot be arrived at by theorem, and she has no immediately recognizable allies. To contain and to be blocked from fulfilling so mastering
an impulse is, finally, punishment and promise enough, as Lawrence
indicates in the marvelous passage in which Ursula has her heart-
stopping encounter with the stampeding horses, hallucination or
reality:

> She knew they had not gone, she knew they awaited her still. But
> she went on over the log bridge that their hoofs had churned and
> drummed, she went on, knowing things about them. She was aware of
> their breasts gripped, clenched narrow in a hold that never relaxed, she
> was aware of their red nostrils flaming with long endurance, and of their
> haunches, so rounded, so massive, pressing, pressing, pressing to burst
> the grip upon their breasts, pressing forever till they went mad, running
> against the walls of time, and never bursting free. Their great haunches
> were smoothed and darkened with rain. But the darkness and wetness
> of rain could not put out the hard, urgent, massive fire that was locked
> within these flanks, never, never.

The new woman is too strong, and the new man is too weak, the
woman suddenly conscious of long-sleeping powers and the man suddenly confronted with a rival. It is as if, for the new broken reed of a
man like Skrebensky, all the long history of patriarchal Western civilization—its dream of wholeness and community, its exaltation of the
family and of romantic love—has been man's dogged postponement of
woman's inevitable supremacy. It all leads to Skrebensky, totally
dependent, beaten child and rejected lover, hearing his doom on the
final morning-after:

> He tapped at her bedroom door at the last minute. She stood with her
> umbrella in her hand. He closed the door. He did not know what to say.

"Have you done with me?" he asked her at length, lifting his head.
"It isn't me," she said. "You have done with me—we have done with
each other."

He looked at her, at the closed face, which he thought so cruel. And
he knew he could never touch her again. His will was broken, he was
seared, but he clung to the life of his body.

"Well, what have I done?" he asked, in a rather querulous voice.

"I don't know," she said, in the same dull, feelingless voice. "It is
finished. It has been a failure."

In this contest—though Skrebensky thinks otherwise—there is no
kindness and cruelty, only life and death, all and nothing; the issue is
beyond the condescensions of charity, and the time is very late. There
must be, somewhere, men to face up to the new dispensation: men
like Tom Brangwen, who did much and might have done more had
he known better what had overtaken him. Anna, in paralyzing con-
tempt of Will when he tried to assert an authority he had already
yielded by his unmanly surrender to her flesh, cried out that her step-
father "could put a dozen of you in his pipe and push them down
with his finger-end." The new woman is strong in her power to wound
and even to kill man's spirit if she has no male counterforce to match
her. Yet life somehow continuously renews itself: in a time of human
degradation, the unique powers of woman have at last asserted themselves; and such powers, coming so unexpectedly out of the very
sources of life, cannot be without a commensurate object and response.
What remains, in the compulsive ugliness of modern industrialism, as
all values except those preservable by the conscious individual are
swept away, is promise:

> In everything she saw she grasped and groped to find the creation of
> the living God, instead of the old, hard barren form of bygone living.
> Sometimes great terror possessed her. Sometimes she lost touch, she lost
> her feeling, she could only know the old horror of the husk which bound
> in her and all mankind. They were all in prison, they were all going
> mad.
>
> She saw the stiffened bodies of the colliers, which seemed already en-
> closed in a coffin, she saw their unchanging eyes, the eyes of those
> who are buried alive: she saw the hard, cutting edges of the new houses,
> which seemed to spread over the hillside in their insentient triumph,
> the triumphs of horrible, amorphous angles and straight lines, the ex-
> pression of corruption triumphant and unopposed, corruption so pure
> that it is hard and brittle: she saw the dun atmosphere over the black-
> ened hills opposite, the dark blotches of houses, slate roofed and
> amorphous, the old church-tower standing up in hideous obsoleteness
> above raw new houses on the crest of the hill, the amorphous, brittle,
> hard edged new houses advancing from Beldover to meet the corrupt
> new houses from Lethley, the houses of Lethley advancing to mix with

the houses of Hainor, a dry, brittle, terrible corruption spreading over the face of the land, and she was sick with a nausea so deep that she perished as she sat. And then, in the blowing clouds, she saw a band of faint irridescence colouring in faint colours a portion of the hill. And forgetting, startled, she looked for the hovering colour and saw a rainbow forming itself. In one place it gleamed fiercely, and, her heart anguished with hope, she sought the shadow of iris where the bow should be. Steadily the colour gathered, mysteriously, from nowhere, it took presence upon itself, there was a faint, vast rainbow. The arc bended and strengthened itself till it arched indomitable, making great architecture of light and colour and the space of heaven, its pedestals luminous in the corruption of new houses on the low hill, its arch the top of heaven.

And the rainbow stood on the earth. She knew that the sordid people who crept hard-scaled and separate on the face of the world's corruption were living still, that the rainbow was arched in their blood and would quiver to life in their spirit, that they would cast off their horny covering of disintegration, that new, clean, naked bodies would issue to a new germination, to a new growth, rising to the light and the wind and the clean rain of heaven. She saw in the rainbow the earth's new architecture, the old, brittle corruption of houses and factories swept away, the world built up in a living fabric of Truth, fitting to the overarching heaven.

The pledge of the future is Ursula's knowledge of what is terrible about the present, and her knowledge derives from a power of passion which must at length be consummated because it would otherwise have had no cause to spring into being. Dostoievsky called the Russians the "god-bearing" people, those who carry the secret of life within them and preserve it for that remote apocalypse when all the world will be fit to receive it. At the conclusion of *The Rainbow* Ursula is the single god-bearing person left in the world. It is a tribute to the prodigious optimism and persuasiveness of Lawrence's vision that the secret she holds seems worth the keeping till the world is fit to receive it.

PART TWO

Interpretations

The First and Second Generation

by H. M. Daleski

I

The opening pages of *The Rainbow* are not only an impassioned prose poem designed to evoke the traditional way of life at the Marsh Farm, nor do they only point to the rhythmic principle underlying the organization of the novel; they are a concentrated, introductory statement of theme. The description of the seasons, for instance, is couched in terms which make it clear that the activity of nature is both a reflection and an affirmation of the fundamental desires of men and women—the desires that Lawrence is to depict:

> But heaven and earth was teeming around them, and how should this cease? They felt the rush of the sap in spring, they knew the wave which cannot halt, but every year throws forward the seed to begetting, and, falling back, leaves the young-born on the earth. They knew the intercourse between heaven and earth, sunshine drawn into the breast and bowels, the rain sucked up in the daytime, nakedness that comes under the wind in autumn, showing the birds' nests no longer worth hiding. Their life and interrelations were such; feeling the pulse and body of the soil, that opened to their furrow for the grain, and became smooth and supple after their ploughing, and clung to their feet with a weight that pulled like desire, lying hard and unresponsive when the crops were to be shorn away . . .

The last sentence of this passage describes the relationship that is established between the Brangwen forebears and the earth; it is also a concise analogue of the sort of responses both Tom and Will encounter in their sexual relations with Lydia and Anna.

"The First and Second Generation" (Editor's title). From The Forked Flame *by H. M. Daleski (London: Faber and Faber, Ltd.; Evanston: Northwestern University Press, 1965), pp. 79–106. Reprinted by permission of the publishers. The pages reprinted here are only part of the chapter entitled "'Two in One': The Second Period."*

The imagery of the passage, which reflects Lawrence's conviction that "everything that is, is either male or female or both," also suggests that it is desirable to read *The Rainbow* with the Hardy essay in mind:[1] the essay draws our attention to significances which are central to Lawrence's purpose, though they have not generally been appreciated. The opening description continues, in part:

> . . . the limbs and the body of the men were impregnated with the day, cattle and earth and vegetation and the sky, the men sat by the fire and their brains were inert, as their blood flowed heavy with the accumulation from the living day.
>
> The women were different. On them too was the drowse of blood-intimacy, calves sucking and hens running together in droves, and young geese palpitating in the hand while the food was pushed down their throttle. But the women looked out from the heated, blind intercourse of farm-life, to the spoken world beyond. They were aware of the lips and the mind of the world speaking and giving utterance, they heard the sound in the distance, and they strained to listen.
>
> It was enough for the men, that the earth heaved and opened its furrows to them. . . . So much warmth and generating and pain and death did they know in their blood, earth and sky and beast and green plants, so much exchange and interchange they had with these, that they lived full and surcharged, their senses full fed, their faces always turned to the heat of the blood, staring into the sun, dazed with looking towards the source of generation, unable to turn round.
>
> But the woman wanted another form of life than this, something that was not blood-intimacy. Her house faced out from the farm-buildings and fields, looked out to the road and the village with church and Hall and the world beyond. She stood to see the far-off world of cities and governments and the active scope of man, the magic land to her, where secrets were made known and desires fulfilled. She faced outwards to where men moved dominant and creative, having turned their back on the pulsing heat of creation, and with this behind them, were set out to discover what was beyond, to enlarge their own scope and range and freedom; whereas the Brangwen men faced inwards to the teeming life of creation, which poured unresolved into their veins.

F. R. Leavis adduces this passage as evidence of how absurd it is to think of Lawrence as "the prophet of the Dark Gods," for it shows that "the life of 'blood-intimacy'" is seen as "something to be transcended."[2] It also suggests, I believe, that the long line of Brangwen

---

[1] Lawrence began the essay in September 1914 (*Letters*, ed. Huxley, p. 208), that is to say, at about the time he began the final draft of *The Rainbow*.

[2] *D. H. Lawrence: Novelist*, p. 99. Despite the clear purport of the passage and despite Leavis's insistence, Lawrence's views in the matter are still misunderstood.

men have failed to realize their "man-being." With their brains inert, they have failed to turn "the accumulation from the living day" to account, to go beyond "the pulsing heat of creation" onward to ut- terance and "the active scope of man." In other words, the disposition of the Brangwen men is essentially female.[3] In consequence the Brang- wen women are not fulfilled; their yearnings for the outside world are only vicariously satisfied. Instead of a living interchange with their husbands, instead of their husbands being the reckless voyagers into the unknown who come back to them and complete them, it is the people of the Hall who provide them with "their own Odyssey," who bring "Penelope and Ulysses before them." Graham Hough com- ments on the unfulfilled aspirations of the Brangwen women, but then he complains that the theme "apparently announced" at the beginning of the novel disconcertingly "disappears" and "we are con- cerned with Tom Brangwen's marriage to a Polish lady." [4] It seems to me, however, that if the significance of the opening pages is taken, we are in fact prepared for the development of Lawrence's theme. The highest kind of married fulfilment is dependent on both the man and the woman extending their being to the utmost, on their reconciling, that is to say, their male and female components (as these are defined in the Hardy essay), and as a result of the tension between these com- ponents, on their transcending the limitations of either. And what is true of the individual struggle for fullness of being is true of the effort of both man and woman to come together in marriage. It takes, as Lawrence shows us, three generations to produce a genuine individual, but Ursula, in *The Rainbow* at any rate, does not find a man who can match and complete her achievement. It is the men, as the opening pages emphasize, that have the longest road to travel.

After the suggestion of the settled continuity of life on the Marsh Farm, it should also be noted that Lawrence begins his actual chronicle by referring to the momentous changes which take place in the valley. For the previous generations of Brangwen men the twin supports of life have been the church and the land:

> Whenever one of the Brangwens in the fields lifted his head from his
> work, he saw the church-tower at Ilkeston in the empty sky. So that

---

S. L. Goldberg, for instance, suggests that "the Brangwens' life" is desiderated as "the image of a human norm." "*The Rainbow:* Fiddle-Bow and Sand," *Essays in Criticism,* 11 (October 1961), 420.

[3] Cf. "In every creature, the mobility, the law of change, is found exemplified in the male; the stability, the conservatism, is found in the female. In woman man finds his root and establishment. In man woman finds her exfoliation and flores- cence. The woman grows downwards, like a root, towards the centre and the dark- ness and the origin. The man grows upwards, like the stalk, towards discovery and light and utterance." "Study of Thomas Hardy," *Phoenix,* p. 515.

[4] *The Dark Sun,* p. 60.

as he turned again to the horizontal land, he was aware of something standing above him and beyond him in the distance.

But, "about 1840," a canal is built "across the meadows of the Marsh Farm" to connect the "newly-opened collieries of the Erewash Valley." As a result the Marsh is "shut off" from Ilkeston (and the church-tower), and when a colliery is sunk on the other side of the canal and the Midland Railway comes down the valley, the "invasion" is complete. For the Brangwens the "something" that stands above and beyond them in the distance is now vaguely menacing:

> As they drove home from town, the farmers of the land met the blackened colliers trooping from the pit-mouth. As they gathered the harvest, the west wind brought a faint, sulphurous smell of pit-refuse burning. As they pulled the turnips in November, the sharp clink-clink-clink-clink-clink of empty trucks shunting on the line, vibrated in their hearts with the fact of other activity going on beyond them.

The ugly fact of the growth of industrialism is not directly alluded to again until three generations have passed and Ursula is a young woman, but it is a fundamental concern of the novel. The life of the individual is organically connected not only with the universe in which he lives but with the life of his fellows, and it is not coincidence that Lawrence begins his account of the childhood of Tom Brangwen in the eighteen-forties. It is in relation to the establishment of the collieries near the Marsh that we are tacitly asked to note, in Tom, a deviation from the traditional attitudes and responses to life of the Brangwen men. Furthermore, such a deviation necessitates an adjustment of the old relation between men and women. *The Rainbow,* indeed, marks the beginning of a search for a *new* relation—a search which, in terms of the defined interests of the two novels, is theoretically brought to a successful conclusion in *Women in Love* but which remained the impetus behind Lawrence's work till the end of his life.

Tom is at once both like his male ancestors and different from them. He has the same sort of nature: when he is at school his "feelings" are said to be more "discriminating" than those of the other boys, and he is "more sensuously developed, more refined in instinct than they," but when it comes to "mental things" he is a "fool." As he grows up he feels that, like the earlier Brangwens, he too is held to the Marsh by a "very strong root," but he is not turned inward in the drowse of blood-intimacy to the same extent as they. When, after an escapade with a girl, he meets "her own man" who turns out to be a fine-mannered foreigner, his dissatisfactions with the life he knows are sharply focused. Unlike the Brangwen women, imaginative participation in the life of others is not sufficient to reconcile him to a more circumscribed life for himself. He "[baulks] the mean enclosure of reality, [standing] stubbornly like a bull at a gate, refusing to re-enter the well-known round of his own life," and he decides that there is nothing in the world of Cossethay and Ilkeston that he wants. What he wants is "an intimacy with fine-textured, subtle-mannered people such as the foreigner at Matlock, and . . . the satisfaction of a voluptuous woman." These desires give promise of being simultaneously fulfilled when he woos and wins the Polish lady, Lydia Lensky.

Tom's marriage to Lydia, judged by the values implied in the opening section of the book, represents both a substantial achievement and an ultimate limitation. It marks a break with the old Brangwen inertness—"That's her," says Tom when he sees Lydia for the first time—and, symbolically, it is an attempt to establish contact with the world outside the Marsh Farm and Cossethay: "It was to him a profound satisfaction that she was a foreigner." That is to say, the marriage represents Tom's movement towards the unknown, and, when Lydia agrees to marry him, the emotional consummation of the marriage is presented in terms of his rebirth:

> He turned and looked for a chair, and keeping her still in his arms, sat down with her close to him, to his breast. Then, for a few seconds, he went utterly to sleep, asleep and sealed in the darkest sleep, utter, extreme oblivion.
>
> From which he came to gradually, always holding her warm and close upon him, and she as utterly silent as he, involved in the same oblivion, the fecund darkness.
>
> He returned gradually, but newly created, as after a gestation, a new birth, in the womb of darkness. Aerial and light everything was, new as a morning, fresh and newly-begun . . .

But the marriage represents a limitation of Tom's development in that it is not the beginning of a further quest into the unknown, into the man's world of action and utterance and discovery, but the end. Nor does he come to Lydia as a man who has achieved fullness of being in his own right: however much he argues that he is "good enough by himself," that he is a man who can stand alone, "he must, in the starry multiplicity of the night humble himself, and admit and know that without her he [is] nothing." F. R. Leavis considers that Tom is "the full complex human psyche, with all its potentialities," [5] but I think we are intended to regard him as essentially a creature of the dark, as a man who aspires towards the light—who aspires, that is to say, to realize his "man-being"—but who cannot, unaided, incorporate the light in a unified self. That, I take it, is the symbolic force of the scene in which Tom, about to propose to Lydia, stands in

the darkness outside her home, watching her for a long time through
the lighted window before he enters the kitchen—as the play of light
and darkness in the following passage and the phrase "invasion from
the night" suggest:

> "Good-evening," she said. "I'll just come in a minute."
> A change went quickly over her face; she was unprepared. She
> looked down at him as he stood in the light from the window, hold-
> ing the daffodils, the darkness behind. In his black clothes she again
> did not know him. She was almost afraid.
> But he was already stepping on to the threshold, and closing the
> door behind him. She turned into the kitchen, startled out of herself
> by this invasion from the night. He took off his hat, and came towards
> her. Then he stood in the light, in his black clothes and his black
> stock, hat in one hand and yellow flowers in the other. She stood
> away, at his mercy, snatched out of herself. She did not know him,
> only she knew he was a man come for her. She could only see the
> dark-clad man's figure standing there upon her, and the gripped fist
> of flowers. She could not see the face and the living eyes.

Lydia, too, is strikingly different from the traditional Brangwen
women. It is not merely that she is a lady and a foreigner; she represents a new conception of "woman-being." Unlike the Brangwen
women, who only "looked out" to the "spoken world beyond," who
"stood to see the far-off world of cities and governments and the active
scope of man," Lydia has herself been part of that world—and she
recoils from it. To the end of her life she resents the fact that her first
husband, a Polish surgeon and revolutionary, simply "incorporated
her in his ideas as if she were not a person herself, as if she were just
his aide-de-camp, or part of his baggage, or one among his surgical
appliances." Looking back on her first marriage, she realizes that to
Lensky she existed only as "one of the baser or material conditions
necessary for his welfare in prosecuting his ideas, of nationalism, of
liberty, of science," but when his work failed and he believed that
"everything had failed" and "stiffened, and died," she rebelled: "The
individual effort might fail, but not the human joy. She belonged to
the human joy." Bereaved of her husband, she experiences a sort of
living death, in which for a long time she remains "blotted safely
away from living," but her responsiveness to the tenacious existence
of some snowdrops which she watches is a prelude to her own spiritual
rebirth: she moves "outside the enclosure of darkness." It is Tom who
is the fertilizing influence in her regeneration. When she meets him,
"the stranger who [is] not a gentleman yet who [insists] on coming
into her life," the "pain of a new birth in herself [strings] all her veins

to a new form. She would have to begin again, to find a new being, a new form, to respond to that blind, insistent figure standing over against her."

The coming together of Tom and Lydia, then, is the occasion for a limited but perceptible movement towards something like true male-female polarity as envisaged in the Hardy essay. Lydia is awakened through Tom to a life of the senses; she represents for Tom a vital connection with the unknown. But because Tom is not sufficiently a "man"—in the sense previously defined—because he both yearns for the unknown and is afraid of it, their relationship is strained.

The fact that Tom attaches a special, extra-personal significance to his relationship with Lydia is the cause of their initial marital dissension. When they "[have] their hour," it is true, he "[buries] himself in the depths of her in an inexhaustible exploration," but for the most part he resents their difference of background the more acutely he realizes that even physically Lydia remains beyond him, that he cannot bring her, the unknown, into a personal relationship with himself: ". . . when they went to bed, he knew that he had nothing to do with her. She was back in her childhood, he was a peasant, a serf, a servant, a lover, a paramour, a shadow, a nothing. . . . And gradually he grew into a raging fury against her." But, at the same time, the fierceness of his desire for her is unappeasable just because the only contact he can make with her strangeness is physical. Consequently, when she turns away from him during the months of her pregnancy, "his existence [is] annulled"; and even after the birth of their child, when she "[comes] to him again, with the same lifting of her mouth as had driven him almost mad with trammelled passion at first," her passion dies down before his and he has to "begin the bitter lesson, to abate himself, to take less than he wanted." His dissatisfaction leads him to turn to Anna for "her sympathy and her love" until soon they are "like lovers, father and child"; and it shows itself in a renewed longing to "clamber out" of the mud of his own existence to the sort of "visionary polite world" he encounters when he visits his brother's mistress. Though he tries to allay his disquiet, he feels "a prisoner, sitting safe and easy and unadventurous" at the Marsh.

What Lawrence does, then, in his portrayal of the marriage is to assert his own characteristic belief in the inevitability, even in the necessity, of conflict between man and wife, and at the same time to indicate that the intensity of the struggle between Tom and Lydia is due to the special nature of the demands he makes on her. After they have been married for about two years, however, their difficulties are suddenly resolved. The passage which describes the cessation of their conflict is long and obscure, but it is centrally important:

"My dear!" she said. He knew she spoke a foreign language.

The fear was like bliss in his heart. He looked down. Her face was shining, her eyes were full of light, she was awful. He suffered from the compulsion to her. She was the awful unknown. He bent down to her, suffering, unable to let go, unable to let himself go, yet drawn, driven. She was now the transfigured, she was wonderful, beyond him. He wanted to go. But he could not as yet kiss her. He was himself apart. Easiest he could kiss her feet. But he was too ashamed for the actual deed, which were like an affront. She waited for him to meet her, not to bow before her and serve her. She wanted his active participation, not his submission. She put her fingers on him. And it was torture to him, that he must give himself to her actively, participate in her, that he must meet and embrace and know her, who was other than himself. There was that in him which shrank from yielding to her, resisted the relaxing towards her, opposed the mingling with her, even whilst he most desired it. He was afraid, he wanted to save himself.

There were a few moments of stillness. Then gradually, the tension, the withholding relaxed in him, and he began to flow towards her. She was beyond him, the unattainable. But he let go his hold on himself, he relinquished himself, and knew the subterranean force of his desire to come to her, to be with her, to mingle with her, losing himself to find her, to find himself in her. He began to approach her, to draw near.

His blood beat up in waves of desire. He wanted to come to her, to meet her. She was there, if he could reach her. The reality of her who was just beyond him absorbed him. Blind and destroyed, he pressed forward, nearer, nearer, to receive the consummation of himself, be received within the darkness which should swallow him and yield him up to himself. If he could come really within the blazing kernel of darkness, if really he could be destroyed, burnt away till he lit with her in one consummation, that were supreme, supreme.

Their coming together now, after two years of married life, was much more wonderful to them than it had been before. It was the entry into another circle of existence, it was the baptism to another life, it was the complete confirmation. . . .

Anna's soul was put at peace between them. She looked from one to the other, and she saw them established to her safety, and she was free. She played between the pillar of fire and the pillar of cloud in confidence, having the assurance on her right hand and the assurance on her left. She was no longer called upon to uphold with her childish might the broken end of the arch. Her father and her mother now met to the span of the heavens, and she, the child, was free to play in the space beneath, between.

The subtle distinctions drawn in this passage make it difficult to follow how it is that Tom suddenly ceases to be "the broken end of the arch," but in terms of the foregoing discussion I think the change in

him is registered convincingly. When Lydia appeals to him, the bliss-
ful fear he feels is of "the awful unknown," and his "compulsion to
her" is his obsessive desire to seize hold of "the beyond" through
her, to subdue the unknown to the known—in the flesh. But, after
two years of marriage, the knowledge that the unknown cannot be
conquered in this way, that she will always remain "other than himself" is "torture" to him. The decisive change comes with his sudden
acceptance of her "otherness," with his recognition that she is "beyond
him," and "unattainable," not to be subdued. When he finally "re-
linquishes himself," he lets go of a self that is accustomed to seeking
its own expansion through her and that is consequently denied satisfaction. He also lets go of a self that "[opposes] the mingling with
her," that is tightly clenched in a desire "to save himself," to preserve
his own distinct identity. But paradoxically, and the phraseology is
suggestive of a mystical illumination, the moment he "loses" himself,
the moment he overcomes his fear and willingly allows the intact self
to be "destroyed," he "finds himself in her." Lawrence, indeed, here
shows how the opposed desires to preserve the self and to yield to
the beloved can be reconciled. . . .

In the newness of his revelation Tom is absorbed by "the reality of
her who [is] just beyond him"; that is to say, for the first time she
becomes a woman to him—she is no longer "the beyond" who happens
to be a woman, but a woman who is the beyond. We remember the
accusation that Lydia makes just prior to the passage quoted: "You
come to me as if it was for nothing, as if I was nothing there. When
Paul came to me, I *was* something to him—a woman, I was. To you I
am nothing—it is like cattle—or nothing—" Their coming together,
then, is the result of Tom's religious submission to the sexual mystery
—their union is both a "baptism" and a "confirmation"—and it is
a submission that involves his final acceptance of the unknown as
the unknown, to be met with through Lydia but not to be ravaged.
Tom, moreover, not only "loses" himself to find himself and to find
her as a woman; it is also justifiable, I think, to regard this as the
moment that Lydia, with his help, begins to find *herself:* many years
later, when he is dead, she reflects that she loved him for having
"given her being. . . . She was very glad she had come to her own
self. She was grateful to Brangwen."

In the last paragraph of the quoted passage the rainbow symbol is
used to suggest the nature of the relationship that is finally established
between Tom and Lydia. The rainbow is one of many symbols that
Lawrence employs to convey his sense of unity in a dualistic universe:
uniting heaven and earth (and we remember "the intercourse between
heaven and earth" that figures so prominently in the opening pages
of the novel), in a meeting of sun and water, it is the "two in one."

As John Middleton Murry has pointed out, it has the same meaning as the crown which relates the lion and the unicorn as a "symbol of their unity in division," or as the Holy Ghost which relates the dual nature of God.[6] As applied to Tom and Lydia, it suggests their achievement of an abiding relationship in which the differences between man and woman are not eliminated but are supplely tensed in a balance of responsive forces. But this, according to Lawrence's views, is surely no more than a *sine qua non* of marriage, a reduction of the rainbow to its minimal symbolic sense. The analogy between the rainbow and symbols such as the crown and the Holy Ghost makes it clear that ideal marriage is based on an altogether wider and more inclusive relationship than that attained by Tom and Lydia:

> There must be marriage of body in body, and of spirit in spirit, and Two-in-One. And the marriage in the body must not deny the marriage in the spirit, for that is blasphemy against the Holy Ghost; and the marriage in the spirit shall not deny the marriage in the body, for that is blasphemy against the Holy Ghost. But the two must be for ever reconciled, even if they must exist on occasions apart one from the other.[7]

Tom and Lydia can hardly be said to be married "in the spirit." What their marriage amounts to is a marriage on "female" terms— as the following passage implies:

> They were a curious family, a law to themselves, separate from the world, isolated, a small republic set in invisible bounds. The mother was quite indifferent to Ilkeston and Cossethay, to any claims made on her from outside . . .
> To this she had reduced her husband. He existed with her entirely indifferent to the general values of the world. Her very ways, the very mark of her eyebrows were symbols and indication to him. There, on the farm with her, he lived through a mystery of life and death and creation, strange, profound ecstasies and incommunicable satisfactions, of which the rest of the world knew nothing; which made the pair of them apart and respected in the English village, for they were also well-to-do.

Lydia, it is seen, becomes the first pronouncedly "female" Brangwen woman at the Marsh, indifferent to the outside world and separate from it, living predominantly through her senses. But the effect she has on her husband is reductive—the word, in the light of Tom's original aspirations, is significant. The sexual fulfillment Tom finds with Lydia is the sustaining validation of his life; it even (as the passage quoted below confirms) affords him intimations of immortality;

[6] *Son of Woman*, p. 101.
[7] "Study of Thomas Hardy," *Phoenix*, p. 475.

but he is reduced in his "man-being." In the end he slips back into a submersion in the physical immediacies and mysteries of farm life that characterized the lives of his father and grandfather before him— and against which he initially revolted. Tom's life, therefore, is both a success and a failure; and the sense of failure, the consciousness of a narrow-dimensioned limitation of life, gnaws at and undermines the rooted solidity of his success:

> What was missing in his life, that, in his ravening soul, he was not satisfied? He had had that friend at school, his mother, his wife, and Anna? What had he done? He had failed with his friend, he had been a poor son; but he had known satisfaction with his wife, let it be enough; he loathed himself for the state he was in over Anna [i.e., over Anna's marriage]. Yet he was *not* satisfied. It was agony to know it.
>
> Was his life nothing? Had he nothing to show, no work? He did not count his work, anybody could have done it. What had he known, but the long, marital embrace with his wife! Curious, that this was what his life amounted to! At any rate, it was something, it was eternal. He would say so to anybody, and be proud of it. He lay with his wife in his arms, and she was still his fulfilment, just the same as ever. And that was the be-all and the end-all. Yes, and he was proud of it.
>
> But the bitterness, underneath, that there still remained an un-satisfied Tom Brangwen, who suffered agony because a girl cared nothing for him. He loved his sons—he had them also. But it was the further, the creative life with the girl, he wanted as well. Oh, and he was ashamed. He trampled himself to extinguish himself.

II

In the second generation man and woman come together through a reversal of the extra-sexual impulse which moves Tom to woo Lydia. It is the man, Will Brangwen, who appears as a "stranger" in Anna's world when he comes to Ilkeston to work in a lace factory. It is Anna who turns to him in the hope of enlarging her experience: "In him the bounds of her experience were transgressed: he was the hole in the wall, beyond which the sunshine blazed on an outside world." Will, moreover, seems to have the capacity, which Tom does not possess, for a creative self-fulfilment. Though his "curious head" reminds Anna of "some animal, some mysterious animal that lived in the darkness under the leaves and never came out, but which lived vividly, swift and intense," and though he is "only half articulate," he comes to utterance in his wood-carving: it is "a passion for him to have the chisel under his grip." When he meets Anna he is carving the Creation of Eve, and under the impetus of his newly awakened love he is

"at last able to create the new, sharp body of his Eve." It is not only
the creation of Eve which is at issue, however; in the developing
drama of the relationship between Will and Anna we are implicitly
invited to observe whether marriage will prove to be a creative release
for him.

In fact, the physical revelations of marriage overwhelm him. The
honeymoon frees his sensual self, but it is the beginning of a process
which leads to the incarceration of his social being:

> One day, he was a bachelor, living with the world. The next day, he
> was with her, as remote from the world as if the two of them were
> buried like a seed in darkness. Suddenly, like a chestnut falling out of
> a burr, he was shed naked and glistening on to a soft, fecund earth,
> leaving behind him the hard rind of worldly knowledge and ex-
> perience . . .

The images in this passage are interesting. It is from the darkness
of the womb that Will and Anna emerge, reborn in the flesh, like
Tom and Lydia before them. But if the chestnut simile reinforces
this idea, it also points to the fact that, for Will, falling from the burr
is—for many years—a final consummation, a ripening which detaches
him from the outside world and leaves him on the fecund earth where
he is content to stay. Though he at first feels that there is "something
unmanly" about his exclusive preoccupation with Anna, it is he who
resents her eventual readiness "to enjoy again a return to the outside
world. . . . He wanted to go on, to go on as they were. He wanted
to have done with the outside world, to declare it finished for ever."

Their first violent quarrel is an expression of the fundamental difference between them in regard to the limits of an absorption in each
other:

> "Can't you do anything?" she said, as if to a child, impatiently.
> "Can't you do your wood-work?"
> "Where shall I do it?" he asked, harsh with pain.
> "Anywhere."
> How furious that made him.
> "Or go for a walk," she continued. "Go down to the Marsh. Don't
> hang about as if you were only half there."
> He winced and hated it. He went away to read. Never had his soul
> felt so flayed and uncreated.
> And soon he must come down again to her. His hovering near her,
> wanting her to be with him, the futility of him, the way his hands
> hung, irritated her beyond bearing. She turned on him blindly and
> destructively, he became a mad creature, black and electric with fury.
> The dark storms rose in him, his eyes glowed black and evil, he was
> fiendish in his thwarted soul.
> There followed two black and ghastly days, when she was set in

anguish against him, and he felt as if he were in a black, violent under-world, and his wrists quivered murderously. And she resisted him. He seemed a dark, almost evil thing, pursuing her, hanging on to her, burdening her. She would give anything to have him removed.

"You need some work to do," she said. "You ought to be at work. Can't you *do* something?"

The fact that Anna talks to Will "as if to a child" effectively indicates the cause of her anger: what she resents is the smothering totality of his unmanly dependence on her, and she fights for the right to be left alone when she wishes, to have an existence apart from him. But Will is immoderately and insatiably compelled to her, and when he is not with her he is annulled—he feels "flayed and uncreated." As I shall try to show, the conflict between them—the necessary battle between male and female—has various manifestations, but it is this initial dispute which is at its centre.

Will, for instance, begins to realize that she does not respect him as a man: "She only respected him as far as he was related to herself. For what he was, beyond her, she had no care. She did not care for what he represented in himself." It is, of course, precisely because Will has ceased to represent anything beyond her that Anna fails to respect him, but this leads him only the more arrogantly to claim consideration as her husband. He asserts his position as "master of the house" and as "the captain of the ship," but Anna is not submissive:

It began well, but it ended always in war between them, till they were both driven almost to madness. He said, she did not respect him. She laughed in hollow scorn of this. For her it was enough that she loved him.

"Respect what?" she asked.

But he always answered the wrong thing. And though she cudgelled her brains, she could not come at it.

"Why don't you go on with your wood-carving?" she said. "Why don't you finish your Adam and Eve?"

But she did not care for the Adam and Eve, and he never put an-other stroke to it. She jeered at the Eve, saying, "She is like a little marionette. Why is she so small? You've made Adam as big as God, and Eve like a doll."

"It is impudence to say that Woman was made out of Man's body," she continued, "when every man is born of woman. What impudence men have, what arrogance!"

In a rage one day, after trying to work on the board, and failing, so that his belly was a flame of nausea, he chopped up the whole panel and put it on the fire. She did not know. He went about for some days very quiet and subdued after it.

Anna cannot formulate her idea of what it is in Will that she might respect if it were developed, but her reference to his wood-carving reveals the direction of her thoughts. His chopping-up of the panel is therefore of some consequence, though the immediate cause of the destruction is no doubt his angry realization of technical failure. It is a symbolic act: many years pass before Will again turns to creative work, and the burning of the panel is in a way a self-destruction; it signifies the extinction, under the stress of a sensual obsession, of the man who appeared capable of utterance. Thereafter, like the phoenix he carved as a butter-stamper for Anna when he was courting her, he has to rise painfully from his own ashes. But his abandonment of the panel also seems to represent his resentful acceptance of the validity of Anna's criticism of the work, his recognition that there is a blatant disproportion in size between the Adam and Eve figures, and it marks the tacit modification of his demands that Anna do him obeisance.

Will's dropping of the overt claim to be master is no more than a modification of his attitude, however, for as has been suggested the claim itself is only one of the manifestations of his refusal to recognize Anna's independence of being. Anna realizes that he seems "to expect her to be part of himself, the extension of his will," and she rouses to fight him off. This aspect of their conflict reflects the collision of elemental forces that stir into motion when they first come together —as the following description of an incident during their courting suggests:

> Corn harvest came on. One evening they walked out through the farm buildings at nightfall. A large gold moon hung heavily to the grey horizon, trees hovered tall, standing back in the dusk, waiting. Anna and the young man went on noiselessly by the hedge, along where the farm-carts had made dark ruts in the grass. They came through a gate into a wide open field where still much light seemed to spread against their faces . . .
>
> They did not want to turn back, yet whither were they to go, towards the moon? For they were separate, single.
>
> "We will put up some sheaves," said Anna. So they could remain there in the broad, open place. . . .
>
> "You take this row," she said to the youth, and passing on, she stooped in the next row of lying sheaves, grasping her hands in the tresses of the oats, lifting the heavy corn in either hand, carrying it, as it hung heavily against her, to the cleared space, where she set the two sheaves sharply down, bringing them together with a faint, keen clash. Her two bulks stood leaning together. He was coming, walking shadowily with the gossamer dusk, carrying his two sheaves. She waited near by. He set his sheaves with a keen, faint clash, next to her sheaves. They rode unsteadily. He tangled the tresses of corn. It hissed like a fountain. He looked up and laughed.

Then she turned away towards the moon, which seemed glowingly
to uncover her bosom every time she faced it. He went to the vague
emptiness of the field opposite, dutifully. . . .

And always, she was gone before he came. As he came, she drew
away, as he drew away, she came. Were they never to meet? Gradually
a low, deep-sounding will in him vibrated to her, tried to set her in
accord, tried to bring her gradually to him, to a meeting, till they should
be together, till they should meet as the sheaves that swished together. . . .

Till at last, they met at the shock, facing each other, sheaves in hand.
And he was silvery with moonlight, with a moonlit, shadowy face that
frightened her. She waited for him.
"Put yours down," she said.
"No, it's your turn." His voice was twanging and insistent.
She set her sheaves against the shock. He saw her hands glisten among
the spray of grain. And he dropped his sheaves and he trembled as he
took her in his arms. He had overtaken her, and it was his privilege, to
kiss her. She was sweet and fresh with the night air, and sweet with the
scent of grain. And the whole rhythm of him beat into his kisses, and
still he pursued her, in his kisses, and still she was not quite overcome.
He wondered over the moonlight on her nose! All the moonlight upon
her, all the darkness within her! All the night in his arms, darkness and
shine, he possessed of it all! All the night for him now, to unfold, to
venture within, all the mystery to be entered, all the discovery to be
made.

The sexual symbolism of this sophisticated pursuit of the bride is
obvious enough, but the obscure second paragraph in the quoted
passage leads to a somewhat different interpretation of the significance
of the incident. What *is* the connection between the moon and
separateness or singleness? If the subsequent description does not
make the connection at once apparent, Lawrence's pronouncements
elsewhere leave us in little doubt as to what it actually is:

The moon, the planet of women, sways us back from our day-self,
sways us back from our real social unison, sways us back, like a retreat-
ing tide, in a friction of criticism and separation and social disintegration. That is woman's inevitable mode, let her words be what they
will. Her goal is the deep, sensual individualism of secrecy and night-
exclusiveness, hostile, with guarded doors. . . .[8]

[8] *Fantasia*, pp. 173–4. Cf. too: "The moon is the centre of our terrestrial individuality in the cosmos. She is the declaration of our existence in separateness.
Save for the intense white recoil of the moon, the earth would stagger towards the
sun. The moon holds us to our own cosmic individuality, as a world individual in
space. She is the fierce centre of retraction, of frictional withdrawal into separateness. She it is who sullenly stands with her back to us, and refuses to meet and
mingle. She it is who burns white with the intense friction of her withdrawal into

What Anna clings to, then, in response to the moon which seems
glowingly to uncover her bosom, is her own individual separateness
of being. And though her night goal is sensual, it is her deepest
"woman-being" which resists the movement towards Will and which
prevents her from being overcome when he finally takes her in his
arms. Will, on the other hand, is impervious to the moon. With the
full force of his "man-being" he is intent on bringing about a meeting. The difference between them even shows itself in the way they
handle the sheaves: her "two bulks" stand "leaning together," but, it
would seem, remain distinguishable; he "tangles" the corn when he
puts his sheaves down, and—in a section of the description not quoted
—he works steadily at "threading his sheaves with hers." The "tan-
gling" and the "threading" are indicative of Will's desire to mingle
and merge with Anna in a union which obliterates all singleness and
separateness; he wants a union in which, in a word, he is "possessed
of" her. And the conflict between them that is foreshadowed in the
cornfield is carried over into their marriage with a ferocious intensity.

The sort of relationship that Anna wants is symbolized by the way
in which she walks home with Will from the Marsh on the evening
that she tells him she is pregnant:

> She put her hand lightly on his arm, out of her far distance. And out
> of the distance, he felt her touch him. They walked on, hand in hand,
> along opposite horizons, touching across the dusk. . . . They continued
> without saying any more, walking . . . hand in hand across the interven-
> ing space, two separate people.

But Will is "afraid" to be alone in his separateness; he wants always
to "be one with her," wants her to come to him "to complete him,"
for he is "ridden by the awful sense of his own limitation." Consequently, he persistently tries to force his will upon her, and she is
uncomfortably aware of "the darkness and other-world . . . in his
soft, sheathed hands." When she comes to him "with her hands full
of love," she receives the "bitter-corrosive shock of his passion upon
her, destroying her in blossom." It is her self-sufficiency that Will
tries to "destroy," and Anna, in a blind effort to save herself, is moved
to an exaggerated assertion of defiance:

> In these days she was oblivious of him. Who was he, to come against
> her? No, he was not even the Philistine, the Giant. He was like Saul
> proclaiming his own kingship. She laughed in her heart. Who was he,
> proclaiming his kingship? She laughed in her heart with pride.
> And she had to dance in exultation beyond him. Because he was in
> the house, she had to dance before her Creator in exemption from the

---

separation, that cold, proud white fire of furious, almost malignant apartness, the
struggle into fierce, frictional separation. . . ." *Ibid.*, pp. 146–7.

man. On a Saturday afternoon, when she had a fire in the bedroom, again she took off her things and danced, lifting her knees and her hands in a slow, rhythmic exulting. He was in the house, so her pride was fiercer. She would dance his nullification, she would dance to her unseen Lord. She was exalted over him, before the Lord.

She heard him coming up the stairs, and she flinched. She stood with the firelight on her ankles and feet, naked in the shadowy, late afternoon, fastening up her hair. He was startled. He stood in the doorway, his brows black and lowering.

"What are you doing?" he said, gratingly. "You'll catch a cold."

And she lifted her hands and danced again, to annul him, the light glanced on her knees as she made her slow, fine movements down the far side of the room, across the firelight. He stood away near the door in blackness of shadow, watching, transfixed. And with slow, heavy movements she swayed backwards and forwards, like a full ear of corn, pale in the dusky afternoon, threading before the firelight, dancing his non-existence, dancing herself to the Lord, to exultation.

He watched, and his soul burned in him. He turned aside, he could not look, it hurt his eyes. Her fine limbs lifted and lifted, her hair was sticking out all fierce, and her belly, big, strange, terrifying, uplifted to the Lord. Her face was rapt and beautiful, she danced exulting before her Lord, and knew no man.

It hurt him as he watched as if he were at the stake. He felt he was being burned alive. The strangeness, the power of her in her dancing consumed him, he was burned, he could not grasp, he could not understand. He waited obliterated. Then his eyes became blind to her, he saw her no more. . . .

F. R. Leavis, in commenting on the conflict between Will and Anna, says: ". . . the nature of the conflict should not, after all, be found defeatingly obscure. Anna, on the face of it, might seem to be the aggressor. The relevant aspect of her has its clear dramatization in the scene that led to the banning of the book; the scene in which she is surprised by Will dancing the defiant triumph of her pregnancy, naked in her bedroom. She is the Magna Mater, the type-figure adverted to so much in *Women in Love* of a feminine dominance that must defeat the growth of any prosperous long-term relation between a man and a woman." [9] This, it seems to me, is fundamentally to mistake the import of Anna's dancing. It is true that Leavis also states that "this dominance in Anna has for its complement a dependence in Will. There are passages that convey to us with the most disturbing force the paradoxical insufferableness to Anna of such a dependence, and its self-frustrating disastrousness";[10] but this qualification hardly offsets the impression he gives that Anna is, in general, the "aggressor"

[9] *D. H. Lawrence: Novelist*, p. 123.
[10] *Ibid.*

in the relationship and, in particular, a target of attack in the description of her dancing. I have already tried to show the extent to which the conflict between Will and Anna derives, ultimately, from *his* imperfections; the quoted passage, I should say, hardly supports the contention that Anna is to be reprehended for her behavior. To begin with, the description itself is not hostile: her movements are "fine," her limbs are "fine," her face is "rapt and beautiful," she sways "like a full ear of corn"—even if her belly is "big, strange, terrifying." But these are only secondary confirmations of a sympathy for her which is implied within the wider context of her relationship with Will. Anna is not the Magna Mater dancing the triumph of her pregnancy; she is a woman asserting her right to singleness, to separateness of being. It is not in her feminine dominance that she exults but in her independence. Such an interpretation accounts, I think, for a number of insistent references in the passage: Anna laughs with pride because she feels she is successfully defying Will's "kingship," not because she is seeking to establish a dictatorship of her own; she dances in exultation "beyond" him, not "over" him; she dances his "nullification" in order to win "exemption" from him. And though Will cannot rationally "understand" what she is doing, intuitively he registers the meaning of the dance. That is why he reacts so strongly. Anna's "separateness" is to him a constant deprivation; he feels defrauded of his own life if he cannot be one with her—hence his sensation of being "burned alive," "consumed," "obliterated." If Anna is criticized at all in this passage it is for the excessiveness of her demonstration, though it is a road of excess which perhaps leads to the palace of wisdom.

The vision of Anna dancing as "a strange, exalted thing having no relation to himself" continually torments Will, but he depends on her too much for her dramatic protest to be instantaneously effective: "If she were taken away, he would collapse as a house from which the central pillar is removed." Will, in other words, is—like Tom before him—the weak, if not quite the broken, end of the arch; and he fights doggedly to prevent everything coming down in ruin about him. It takes a great strength of resistance on Anna's part before he eventually learns what it is "to be able to be alone":

> It was right and peaceful. She had given him a new, deeper freedom. The world might be a welter of uncertainty, but he was himself now. He had come into his own existence. He was born for a second time, born at last unto himself, out of the vast body of humanity. Now at last he had a separate identity, he existed alone, even if he were not quite alone. Before he had only existed in so far as he had relations with another being. Now he had an absolute self—as well as a relative self.

Will, therefore, is reborn twice: first, into the wondering apprehension of his sensual self, and then into the certainty of his "absolute self." Yet his attainment of a separate identity still does not qualify the stultification of his "man-being": he still feels that "the whole of the man's world [is] exterior and extraneous to his own real life with Anna."

At this stage of the marriage Anna is "Anna Victrix," but she is "still . . . not quite fulfilled":

> She had a slight expectant feeling, as of a door half opened. Here she was, safe and still in Cossethay. But she felt as if she were not in Cossethay at all. She was straining her eyes to something beyond. And from her Pisgah mount, which she had attained, what could she see? A faint, gleaming horizon, a long way off, and a rainbow like an archway, a shadow-door with faintly coloured coping above it. Must she be moving thither?
>
> Something she had not, something she did not grasp, could not arrive at. There was something beyond her. But why must she start on the journey? She stood so safely on the Pisgah mountain. . . .
>
> There was another child coming, and Anna lapsed into vague content. If she were not the wayfarer to the unknown, if she were arrived now, settled in her builded house, a rich woman, still her doors opened under the arch of the rainbow, her threshold reflected the passing of the sun and the moon, the great travellers, her house was full of the echo of journeying.
>
> She was a door and a threshold, she herself. Through her another soul was coming, to stand upon her as upon the threshold, looking out, shading its eyes for the direction to take.

The phrase "as of a door half opened" provides a clue to the nature of Anna's discontent. It was to Will, we remember, that she originally turned in the hope of enlarging her experience; he was to be "the hole in the wall, beyond which the sunshine blazed on an outside world." After years of marriage she has to admit that the door is only half-open; she has found sexual fulfilment with him but he stands for nothing beyond her. Consequently, like the Brangwen women of old, she has to strain her eyes to see that which she had hoped to live. And because the denial of this hope functions as so important an element in the marriage, Anna herself does not gain entry to the Promised Land though she has so arduously climbed "her Pisgah mount." All that she is granted is a vision of the rainbow, for if her doors can be said to open "under the arch of the rainbow," the archway is "a long way off . . . a shadow-door." Anna herself is in part to blame for what must be considered an ultimate failure. From the outset she has resisted the unknown, has even resisted contact with it in the sexual mystery: "It was always the unknown, always the unknown, and she clung fiercely to her known self. But the rising flood carried her away." It is partly as a result of her own limitations, therefore, that Anna remains "safe and still in Cossethay," content to relinquish "the adventure to the unknown." No wayfarer herself, she looks to her children to do her journeying for her, and "lapses"— the word is symptomatic of her condition as she placidly proceeds to bear nine children—into a vague physical content.

But first she has one more battle to fight with Will. Previous to this she has attacked his religious beliefs and practices, but this skirmishing is merely the preliminary to the decisive engagement at Lincoln Cathedral:

> [Will] turned his glowing, ecstatic face to [Anna], his mouth opened with a strange, ecstatic grin.
>
> "There she is," he said.
>
> The "she" irritated her. Why "she"? It was "it." What was the cathedral, a big building, a thing of the past, obsolete, to excite him to such a pitch? She began to stir herself to readiness. . . .
>
> In a little ecstasy he found himself in the porch, on the brink of the unrevealed. He looked up to the lovely unfolding of the stone. He was to pass within to the perfect womb.
>
> Then he pushed open the door, and the great, pillared gloom was before him, in which his soul shuddered and rose from her nest. His soul leapt, soared up into the great church. His body stood still, absorbed by the height. His soul leapt up into the gloom, into possession, it reeled, it swooned with a great escape, it quivered in the womb, in the hush and the gloom of fecundity, like seed of procreation in ecstasy.

Anna stirs herself to readiness in intuitive awareness that it is really the old battle between them that is about to be joined—though it takes the guise of a religious quarrel. Tuned to Will as she is, the sight of his "ecstatic" face and his use of the feminine pronoun for the cathedral alert her to the covert significance of his entry into the church. Nathan A. Scott writes: "The Cathedral-arch is obviously a sexual symbol, but it also has more extensive symbolic ramifications which suggest a transcendent world of Mystery, in the attainment of which the idiom of the sex act is merely instrumental and evocative." [11] It seems to me that to regard the sexual imagery as "merely instrumental and evocative" is to miss the point of the ensuing altercation between Will and Anna. His entry into the cathedral is described in terms of the sex act because he approaches the religious mystery with the same craving that he brings to the sexual mystery. The suggestion, indeed, is of a spiritual orgasm in which he "swoons with a great escape" from himself, from the fearsome burden of his lonely singleness, both losing himself in the gloom of the church and taking "possession" of it.

[11] *Rehearsals of Discomposure*, p. 147.

Until Anna intervenes, Will enjoys, in the cathedral, the same sort of "consummation" that he has relentlessly been seeking to find in her. It is as if his rebirth into "separate identity" is annulled, and as if his old desires, secure in the camouflage of religious emotion, triumphantly seize at satisfaction:

> She too was overcome with wonder and awe. She followed him in his progress. Here, the twilight was the very essence of life, the coloured darkness was the embryo of all light, and the day. Here, the very first dawn was breaking, the very last sunset sinking, and the immemorial darkness, whereof life's day would blossom and fall away again, re-echoed peace and profound immemorial silence.
>
> Away from time, always outside of time! Between east and west, between dawn and sunset, the church lay like a seed in silence, dark before germination, silenced after death. Containing birth and death, potential with all the noise and transition of life, the cathedral remained hushed, a great, involved seed, whereof the flower would be radiant life inconceivable, but whose beginning and whose end were the circle of silence. Spanned round with the rainbow, the jewelled gloom folded music upon silence, light upon darkness, fecundity upon death as a seed folds leaf upon leaf and silence upon the root and the flower, hushing up the secret of all between its parts, the death out of which it fell, the life into which it has dropped, the immortality it involves, and the death it will embrace again.
>
> Here in the church, "before" and "after" were folded together, all was contained in oneness. Brangwen came to his consummation. . . .
>
> Here the stone leapt up from the plain of earth, leapt up in a manifold, clustered desire each time, up, away from the horizontal earth, through twilight and dusk and the whole range of desire, through the swerving, the declination, ah, to the ecstasy, the touch, to the meeting and the consummation, the meeting, the clasp, the close embrace, the neutrality, the perfect, swooning consummation, the timeless ecstasy. There his soul remained, at the apex of the arch, clinched in the timeless ecstasy, consummated.

This passage presents Will's experience so sympathetically that only a close scrutiny reveals that Lawrence is not identifying himself with it; and the appearance, at this juncture, of the rainbow symbol makes the greater the temptation to believe that he is. This rainbow, however, is artificial, a compound projection of the cathedral arch and of the "jewelled gloom"; and what it symbolizes is not unity in diversity, the union of a separate heaven and earth, but the attainment of a "oneness" that obliterates all distinction. The decisive image in this respect is the twilight, that which is neither light nor darkness but is "the very essence of life" in the cathedral, and the conclusive concept is the "neutrality" of the final close embrace of the stone. The passage posits the "timeless ecstasy" of an absolute which is insidiously compelling, to which Will surrenders in a surging attempt to merge

himself with it—but to Lawrence it is anathema. The only absolute
that Lawrence is prepared to acknowledge is the "Holy Ghost," that
which relates conflicting forces but does not neutralize them.

Anna's reaction to the cathedral is distinguished from that of Will:

> Her soul too was carried forward to the altar, to the threshold of
> Eternity, in reverence and fear and joy. But ever she hung back in the
> transit, mistrusting the culmination of the altar. She was not to be
> flung forward on the lift and lift of passionate flights, to be cast at last
> upon the altar steps as upon the shore of the unknown. There was a
> great joy and a verity in it. But even in the dazed swoon of the cathedral,
> she claimed another right. The altar was barren, its lights gone out.
> God burned no more in that bush. It was dead matter lying there. She
> claimed the right to freedom above her, higher than the roof. She had
> always a sense of being roofed in.
>
> So that she caught at little things, which saved her from being swept
> forward headlong in the tide of passion that leaps on into the Infinite
> in a great mass, triumphant and flinging its own course. She wanted to
> get out of this fixed, leaping, forward-travelling movement, to rise from
> it as a bird rises with wet, limp feet from the sea, to lift herself as a
> bird lifts its breast and thrusts its body from the pulse and heave of a
> sea that bears it forward to an unwilling conclusion, tear herself away
> like a bird on wings, and in the open space where there is clarity, rise up
> above the fixed, surcharged motion, a separate speck that hangs sus-
> pended, moves this way and that, seeing and answering before it sinks
> again, having chosen or found the direction in which it shall be carried
> forward.
>
> And it was as if she must grasp at something, as if her wings were
> too weak to lift her straight off the heaving motion. So she caught sight
> of the wicked, odd little faces carved in stone, and she stood before
> them arrested.
>
> These sly little faces peeped out of the grand tide of the cathedral
> like something that knew better. They knew quite well, these little
> imps that retorted on man's own illusion, that the cathedral was not ab-
> solute. They winked and leered, giving suggestion of the many things
> that had been left out of the great concept of the church. "However
> much there is inside here, there's a good deal they haven't got in," the
> little faces mocked.
>
> Apart from the lift and spring of the great impulse towards the altar,
> these little faces had separate wills, separate motions, separate knowledge,
> which rippled back in defiance of the tide, and laughed in triumph of
> their own very littleness.
>
> "Oh look!" cried Anna. "Oh look, how adorable, the faces! Look at
> her."
>
> Brangwen looked unwillingly. This was the voice of the serpent in
> his Eden . . .

The characterization of Anna's interjection as "the voice of the
serpent" lends a certain plausibility to John Middleton Murry's inter-

pretation of the scene: "The meaning of all this symbolism is patent. Through the woman, through sex, the spiritual ideal is destroyed; and it is good that it should be destroyed. For the spiritual ideal is partial and false. It is based on the negation of sex, of the mighty principle of life itself." [12] This is not only a distortion of Lawrencean doctrine but of scant relevance to the scene in question. Anna, despite her natural scepticism, despite her belief that the lights of the altar have gone out, is not fighting Will's "spirituality," nor is he a man who places the spirit above the flesh—rather the reverse. What she resents and resists is Will's submission to the overwhelming "oneness" of the cathedral. Characteristically, she asserts the right of the individual to detach himself from the mass, to rise like a bird above the engulfing sea, separate and distinct. And she clings to the gargoyles not because they symbolize female carnality, as Murry suggests, but because—as for Ruskin—they symbolize individual freedom and point to the existence of *"separate* wills, *separate* motions, *separate* knowledge." [13] They also point to the "many things" that have been "left out" of the "grand tide," and reaffirm for Anna the importance of a world beyond the ecstasy—the "open sky" that the cathedral disdains, the "man's world" that Will denies in his exclusive absorption both in her and in the church.

In the dispute over the gargoyles that follows her intervention, Anna emerges victorious (though it should be noted that, in the passage quoted, she too is tacitly criticized for a typical limitation of being, for her heavy reluctance to adventure, her instinctive resistance to being "cast . . . upon the shore of the unknown"). Not only does she herself "[get] free" from the cathedral, she even destroys his passion: "Strive as he would, he could not keep the cathedral wonderful to him." Thereafter Will continues to devote himself to the church next to his house, labouring at works of restoration, but he is "like a lover who knows he is betrayed, but who still loves, whose love is only the more tense." As far as his work at the office is concerned, he

---

[12] *Son of Woman*, p. 81.

[13] A relevant comment on the significance of the gargoyles is to be found in the Hardy essay: ". . . the art produced [all through the medieval period] was the collective, stupendous, emotional gesture of the Cathedrals, where a blind, collective impulse rose into concrete form. It was the profound, sensuous desire and gratitude which produced an art of architecture, whose essence is in utter stability, of movement resolved and centralized, of absolute movement, that has no relationship with any other form, that admits the existence of no other form, but is conclusive, propounding in its sum the One Being of All.

"There was, however, in the Cathedrals, already the denial of the Monism which the Whole uttered. All the little figures, the gargoyles, the imps, the human faces, whilst subordinated within the Great Conclusion of the Whole, still, from their obscurity, jeered their mockery of the Absolute, and declared for multiplicity, polygeny [sic] . . ." *Phoenix*, p. 454.

"[does] not exist"; he "[keeps] himself suspended," and is content to live by Anna's "physical love for him." Like Tom, however, he is painfully aware of "some limit to himself," of "a darkness in him which he *could* not unfold, which would never unfold in him." Anna, on the other hand, "lapses," as previously indicated, into her child-bearing; "every moment" is "full and busy with productiveness" and she feels "like the earth, the mother of everything."

Will's ultimate dissatisfaction with his life is presented in a way that quietly emphasizes the rhythmic movement of the book. As Tom turned to Anna when she was a child, so Will turns to Ursula "for love and for fulfilment," but the repetition is subtly varied. Will encounters in Ursula a determination to "relapse" into "her own separate world of herself," and he frantically fights to dominate her—jumping with her on his back, for instance, from a high canal bridge into the water beneath, or swinging dangerously high with her in a swing-boat at the fair. He also tries to turn from Anna to another woman, making an unsuccessful attempt to seduce a young girl whom he sits next to at a music-hall, but it is clear that it is not a sexual hunger that he is seeking to appease: "She would be small, almost like a child, and pretty. Her childishness whetted him keenly. She would be helpless between his hands."

Anna senses the challenge to her old supremacy, and for the first time she willingly goes to meet the unknown. She waits "for his touch as if he were a marauder who had come in, infinitely unknown and desirable to her," and they begin to live in a renewed "passion of sensual discovery":

> This was what their love had become, a sensuality violent and extreme as death. They had no conscious intimacy, no tenderness of love. It was all the lust and the infinite, maddening intoxication of the senses, a passion of death. . . .

> But still the thing terrified him. Awful and threatening it was, dangerous to a degree, even whilst he gave himself to it. It was pure darkness, also. All the shameful things of the body revealed themselves to him now with a sort of sinister, tropical beauty. All the shameful natural and unnatural acts of sensual voluptuousness which he and the woman partook of together, created together, they had their heavy beauty and their delight. Shame, what was it? It was part of extreme delight. It was that part of delight of which man is usually afraid. Why afraid? The secret, shameful things are most terribly beautiful.

> They accepted shame, and were one with it in their most unlicensed pleasures. It was incorporated. It was a bud that blossomed into beauty and heavy, fundamental gratification.

When we consider this passage in isolation, we can do no more than guess at the nature of the "shameful acts" that Will and Anna "[partake] of together." In the light of Lawrence's later work, however, the phrasing of the description is suggestive: their love has become "a sensuality violent and extreme as death" and it debars "tenderness"; the "secret, shameful things" are not only accepted but are found to be "most terribly beautiful"; their "pleasures" are "unlicensed" as well as "unnatural"; and their "gratification" is "heavy" and "fundamental." The terms used are similar to those employed in *Women in Love* and then again, with a more specific connotation in view of their context, in *Lady Chatterley's Lover,* and I think we can be reasonably confident that one of the practices Will and Anna indulge in is the same as that in which Mellors and Connie engage on their "night of sensual passion." Since I shall argue that Mellors engages in this practice as a means of asserting his manhood and, furthermore, that Lawrence does violence to the character of Connie in making her submit to him, it is worth pointing to some important differences between the two couples. First, we note that Will and Anna "create" their voluptuous sensuality "together," that they are equal partners in the enterprise, and that there is no suggestion here of a slave-like submission on the part of the woman. Anna "[adheres] as little as he to the moral world," even though, for her, this period of their love is merely an interlude in the "sleep of motherhood" from which she does not really wake until she has borne her last child and it is growing up. Second, and this is a crucial difference between Will and Mellors, though Will's passion may seem to be generated by a lust for dominance—"the little creature in Nottingham," we are told, "had but been leading up to this"—he does not attempt in fact to assert his manhood in this way. He seeks, rather, "gratification pure and simple," and *his* "sensuality" sets "another man in him free." The "passion of death," in his case, is a prelude to yet a further rebirth. The "new man" turns to "public life," to a "new activity" for which he is "now created and released": he has "at length, from his profound sensual activity, developed a real purposive self."

Will tries to take a part in "public life" by running a woodwork class in Cossethay. The woodwork class is no doubt a meagre achievement of "man-being," but after the period of his submersion in Anna it is a step forward. As a result of his work, "the house by the yew trees" is placed "in connexion with the great human endeavour at last," and it gains "a new vigour thereby." Later, after twenty years of marriage, Will even returns to his own wood-carving, coming back "almost to the point where he had left off his Adam and Eve panel, when he was courting," wanting once again "to carve things that [are] utterances of himself." But his creative force is spent, and his excited experiments in other mediums are nothing more than moderately successful dabblings. To the end both Anna and Will are not "quite personal, quite defined as individuals."

The Third Generation

by Keith Sagar

The third generation story differs from the first two in that Ursula's "struggles against the confines of her life" take place before marriage. Her disposition is adventurous, eager, naïvely optimistic:

> She wanted to read great, beautiful books, and be rich with them; she wanted to see beautiful things, and have the joy of them for ever; she wanted to know big, free people; and there remained always the want she could put no name to.

We see, through Ursula, what modern society offers, either masquerading as these things or as alternatives to them. Her story is of disillusion, but also of the courage which transcends it, replacing broken dreams not by cynicism or conformity, but by new, more robust and more jealously guarded dreams. Her faith in life is never shaken. If life seems to thwart her, it must be that she has sought the wrong things; rather than ask for less, she will ask even more of it.

Tom and Lydia were rooted at Marsh Farm, where the Brangwens had lived "for generations." They lived in the past—the mellow past of the yeoman farmer—unaffected by the distant sounds of pit and railway. Ursula's first suitor, Anthony Schofield, is very like the young Tom. He offers Ursula a return to the "horizontal" world. Ursula "cannot" accept. It is a question of consciousness:

> She turned away, she turned round from him, and saw the east flushed strangely rose, the moon coming yellow and lovely upon a rosy sky, above the darkening, bluish snow. All this so beautiful, all this so lovely. He did not see it. He was one with it. But she saw it, and was one with it. Her seeing separated them infinitely. . . . She was a traveller on the face of the earth, and he was an isolated creature living in the fulfilment of his own senses.

"The Third Generation" (Editor's title). From The Art of D. H. Lawrence *by Keith Sagar (Cambridge: Cambridge University Press, 1966), pp. 55–68. Reprinted by permission of the author and the publisher. The pages reprinted here are only part of the chapter entitled "The Perfect Medium, 1913–1914," and have been somewhat revised for this volume.*

As the first generation had taken the rhythm of its life from the seasons, the natural cycles of birth, death and fruition, pagan, with only the first glimmer of spiritual aspiration, so the second generation lives within the rhythms of the Church year, and Ursula's young life gladly responds to this cycle, each week turning about the precious Sunday, and each year on Christmas and Easter:

> So the children lived the year of christianity, the epic of the soul of mankind. Year by year the inner, unknown drama went on in them, their hearts were born and came to fulness, suffered on the cross, gave up the ghost, and rose again to unnumbered days, untired, having at least this rhythm of eternity in a ragged, inconsequential life.

But the great drama, at this moment of history, is becoming mechanical, tawdry; it goes the way of Ursula's earlier passion for Romance and her later passion for Knowledge, failing, like them, to match the realities of her experience.

The Brangwen farmers had been only dimly aware of church and hall and school in the distance, always on the perimeter of their consciousness holding out a promise their consciousness could never fully grasp. Will and Anna had set up house in Cossethay, in close proximity to church and school. Later, when Will became Art and Handwork Instructor to the County of Nottingham, they moved to Beldover —"new red-brick suburbia in a grimy, small town." Ursula faces the problems of adjustment and emancipation in a specifically urban and twentieth-century environment. She has to grow into a world which offers no communal fulfilment or aspiration, no civilised life-effort worth taking part in. The first danger is that she will be beaten down by the system; but the second and even greater danger is that she will seek her absolute within her own ego, exploiting others to serve her lusts. Ursula is emancipated and uprooted: she is free as her parents and grandparents were not, but free as a man overboard without a lifebelt is freer than those trapped aboard a sinking ship. In which direction shall she strike out?

> How to act, that was the question? Whither to go, how to become oneself? One was not oneself, one was merely a half-stated question. How to become oneself, how to know the question and the answer of oneself, when one was merely an unfixed something-nothing, blowing about like the winds of heaven, undefined, unstated.

Is she an island unto herself alone; or must she find, outside herself, someone or something worthy of service? It is a specifically modern dilemma, which few of us face with Ursula's honesty and courage.

Ursula is the first "free soul" in the English novel. The structure of this novel must change to accommodate her desperate search for bearings. In the first generation Tom had to extend the boundaries of

the inherited life, which had become oppressive. In the second generation values clashed and modified each other, ending in a compromise
and withdrawal from the struggle. Ursula doggedly persists, veering
away from that from which her soul recoils, moving into unknown
territory with no better guide than the principle of trial and error,
a deep sense of responsibility for her own life, and an indestructible
faith, at the very centre of her, surviving all disillusions, in a world of
"absolute truth and living mystery" within the everyday world, within
herself and all living things. In adolescence, she thinks of this as the
Sunday world, over which the weekday world quickly triumphs,
superficially.

Like Ellie in Shaw's *Heartbreak House,* Ursula is looking for "life
with a blessing," which is what the rainbow specifically symbolises.
Before she finds her true rainbow at the end of the novel, she must
follow several false rainbows—loves and allegiances which do not
bring the liberation she seeks. Her love for Christ, she realises, is
merely a substitute for loving and being loved in the flesh. Yet physical
love in its turn, in the person of Skrebensky, proves unable to satisfy
her: "Between them was the compact of his flesh with hers, in the
hand-clasp." But Skrebensky is not a son of God, not an incarnation
of the mystery, so the sensual compact with him is not also the covenant with God.

To the girlish Ursula, Skrebensky brings "a strong sense of the
outer world": "She laid hold of him at once for her dreams." But the
want that Ursula could put no name to is not to be satisfied by Skrebensky. He is a soldier, responding, in peace time, to such dead ideals
as "nation" and "property." He serves "the highest good of the community," meaning material prosperity. He is "just a brick in the
whole great social fabric":

> His life lay in the established order of things. . . . At the bottom of his
> heart, his self, the soul that aspired and had true hope of self-effectua-
> tion lay as dead, still-born, a dead weight in his womb.

A man must conceive his own soul, bring his self to birth. Ursula
herself has come far enough on this road to recognise Skrebensky as a
nonentity:

> "It seems to me as if you weren't anybody—as if there weren't anybody
> there, where you are. Are you anybody, really? You seem like nothing to
> me."

Lawrence has set himself a difficult enough task in describing the
inner core of a character. But when that core is absent, where the
penetrating vision reveals a mere void, the task is virtually impossible
unless other modes of presentation are also drawn on. Here expanses

of intrusive direct comment from the author and repetitive and over-written symbolic passages draw out interminably the breaking of this butterfly. A negative character can be substantial, as Gerald is to be in *Women in Love*. Skrebensky seems to be a first sketch for Gerald. But he hardly carries his weight in *The Rainbow*.

The incomplete personality can never be the complete lover or husband. The "unknown" is excluded from Skrebensky's world-view, as it is from the "passion" he offers Ursula:

> It was magnificent self-assertion on the part of both of them, he asserted himself before her, he felt himself infinitely male and infinitely irresistible, she asserted herself before him, she knew herself infinitely desirable, and hence infinitely strong. And after all, what could either of them get from such a passion but a sense of his or her own maximum self, in contradistinction to all the rest of life? Wherein was something finite and sad, for the human soul at its maximum wants a sense of the infinite.

We are invited at the outset to compare this relationship with the previous generations. Ursula walks

> where her grandfather had walked with his daffodils to make his proposal, and where her mother had gone with her young husband, walking close upon him as Ursula was now walking upon Skrebensky.

We remember the moonlit stooking scene, where the rhythm of the work carried Will and Anna ever closer until they met "as the sheaves that swish together." Will's "steadied purpose" was more profound than his consciousness and made his proposal part of a wider pattern of creativeness and fruition. The first coming together of Ursula and Skrebensky initiates Ursula only into the release of her own desires and an awareness "of what a kiss might be." His five senses are to be gratified. And she uses him as a mere vehicle for her lust, "a fierce, white, cold passion," which is really a relationship between Ursula and Aphrodite. She annihilates him as a person. He is the necessary medium for her self-contained, uncreative, corrosive lust, burning, poisonous, deadly. They perform a dance of death under the all-pervading moonlight. Ursula, glorying in her triumph, "felt she had now all licence." "Her sexual life flamed to a kind of disease within her," and Skrebensky existed "in her own desire only."

In Skrebensky's absence Ursula turns to the lights and crowds of the town as a haven of tangible values outside the chaos of her own uncreated consciousness:

> All this stir and seethe of lights and people was but the rim, the shores of a great inner darkness and void. She wanted very much to be on the seething, partially illuminated shore, for within her was the void reality of dark space.

But "seethe" as opposed to "glow" in *Sons and Lovers* is a word
which the novel is to define, negatively, through Ursula's consciousness:

> The stupid, artificial, exaggerated town, fuming its lights. It does not
> exist really.

Ursula's disillusion comes largely through her relationship with
Winifred Inger, a scientific humanist:

> Winifred had had a scientific education. She had known many clever
> people. She wanted to bring Ursula to her own position of thought. In
> philosophy she was brought to the conclusion that the human desire is
> the criterion of all truth and all good. Truth does not lie beyond human-
> ity, but is one of the products of the human mind and feeling.

Sexually and educationally, her influence is equally perverted and
deadly. Winifred marries Uncle Tom, a colliery-owner from the min-
ing village of Wiggiston. Tom believes that "living human beings
must be taken and adapted to all kinds of horrors." Life is a squalid
heap of side-shows round the pit, the *raison d'être* of all. After the
nightmare experience of Wiggiston, Ursula is able to reject the God
of the Machine, worshipped by both Uncle Tom and Winifred (in her
case "the impure abstraction and mechanisms of matter").

This experience does not deter Ursula from striving to connect
herself "with the outer, greater world of activity, the man-made
world." Her parents become very real barriers. She is already transcending their values. They shatter her dream of teaching at Kingston-
on-Thames and condemn her to Brinsley Street School, Ilkeston.
There "everything was as in hell, a condition of hard, malevolent system." Ursula's "responsive, personal self" is out of place where teachers
must be "hard, insentient things, that worked mechanically, according to a system." "The whole situation was wrong and ugly." The
education system is part of a subtle death spreading through society.
The boy Williams has a "half-transparent unwholesomeness, rather
like a corpse." His mother has a "sense of being unpleasant to touch,
like something going bad inside." Ursula is shut in with "unliving
spectral people." She must break away from this sunless, lifeless, enclosed form of life. But she will not retreat "into her fields where
she was happy." She will continue to fight for "joy, happiness, and
permanency" within modern industrial society:

> She must have her place in the working world, be a recognised member
> with full rights there. It was more important to her than fields and sun
> and poetry, at this time. But she was only the more its enemy.

Ursula's new identity as Standard Five Teacher gives her independence from her parents:

In coming out and earning her own living she had made a strong, cruel move towards freeing herself.

It is not a matter of female emancipation:

> She had within her the strange, passionate knowledge of religion and living far transcending the limits of the automatic system that contained the vote. But her fundamental organic knowledge had as yet to take form and rise to utterance. . . . She felt that somewhere, in something, she was not free. And she wanted to be. She was in revolt. For once she were free she could get somewhere. Ah, the wonderful, real somewhere that was beyond her, the somewhere that she felt deep, deep inside her.

Lawrence makes this "somewhere" take form and rise to utterance in the closing pages.

Another disillusionment awaits Ursula at the University, where "the religious virtue of knowledge was become a flunkey to the god of material success."

> Always the shining doorway ahead; and then, upon approach, always the shining doorway was a gate into another ugly yard, dirty and active and dead. Always the crest of the hill gleaming ahead under heaven: and then, from the top of the hill only another sordid valley full of amorphous, squalid activity.

Her movement is restricted, her growth stunted, her horizons close in. Anna had been satisfied to hold on to the wide sky and sunlit land as her absolute. This landscape, richly invested with values, remains, nevertheless, the real landscape which is the physical setting of the novel, just as Will's absolute remained incarnate in the solid masonry of cathedrals. But Ursula comes to perceive that "the world in which she lived was like a circle lighted by a lamp":

> . . . Nevertheless the darkness wheeled round about, with grey shadow-shapes of wild beasts, and also with dark shadow-shapes of the angels, whom the light fenced out, as it fenced out the more familiar beasts of darkness.

This is no longer the physical setting, but a psychic landscape which Ursula's soul explores:

> "What do you think you are?" her soul asked of the professor as she sat opposite him in class. "What do you think you are, as you sit there in your gown and your spectacles? You are a lurking, blood-sniffing creature with eyes peering out of the jungle darkness, snuffing for your desires."

She recognises the darkness of her own unconscious not only as the home of hyena and wolf, but of angels "lordly and terrible and not to be denied." The gleam in the eye of the wild beast, the flash of fangs, is also the flash of the sword of angels, for the gleam is the very quick of life. Miraculously, Lawrence brings us back from the psychic drama to the narrative analogy by letting Ursula at college see the same gleam through her microscope as she examines a living cell:

> She looked at the unicellular shadow that lay within the field of light, under her microscope. It was alive. She saw it move—she saw the bright mist of its ciliary activity, she saw the gleam of its nucleus, as it slid across the plane of light. What then was its will? If it was a conjunction of forces, physical and chemical, what held these forces unified, and for what purpose were they unified?
>
> For what purpose were the incalculable physical and chemical activities nodalised in this shadowy, moving speck under her microscope? What was the will which nodalised them and created the one thing she saw? What was its intention? To be itself? Was its purpose just mechanical and limited to itself?
>
> It intended to be itself. But what self? Suddenly in her mind the world gleamed strangely, with an intense light, like the nucleus of the creature under the microscope. Suddenly she had passed away into an intensely-gleaming light of knowledge. She could not understand what it all was. She only knew that it was not limited mechanical energy, nor mere purpose of self-preservation and self-assertion. It was a consummation, a being infinite. To be oneself was a supreme, gleaming triumph of infinity.

But *how* to be oneself?

Despite her earlier dissection of him in the vain hope of finding some intact core, she still holds on to Skrebensky as the key to this puzzle, the next shining doorway:

> She would not admit to herself the chill like a sunshine of frost that came over her. This was he, the key, the nucleus to the new world.

It was again "as if she were a blank wall in his direction, without windows or outgoings." They are enemies come together in a sensual truce.

> Every movement and word of his was alien to her being. . . . He seemed made up of a set of habitual actions and decisions. The vulnerable, variable quick of the man was inaccessible. She knew nothing of it. She could feel the dark, heavy fixity of his animal desire. . . . He wanted something that should be nameless. . . . The same iron rigidity, as if the world were made of steel, possessed her again. It was no use turning with flesh and blood to this arrangement of forged metal.

She sees that Skrebensky is to be associated rather with Doctor Frankstone than with the nucleus, and with Mr. Harby, and Winifred and Uncle Tom, and all other mechanical wills she has met and rejected. At last Ursula has to recognise that love as a matter of personal gratification, as an end in itself, is not enough for her:

Love—love—love—what does it mean—what does it amount to? . . .
As an end in itself, I could love a hundred men, one after the other.
Why should I end with a Skrebensky?

Frieda, who helped to write *The Rainbow* and on whom Ursula is
largely based, comments:

> In the end the man fails Ursula because he has no ideal beyond the old
> existing state, it does not satisfy her nor him. For perfect love you don't
> only have two people, it must include bigger, universal connection. An
> *idea*, something outside themselves, and it is really against individualism.[1]

The crisis comes when, in alliance with a full, dazzling moon, she
challenges him to satisfy her. But the unknown does not emerge from
this experience. Ursula comes no nearer to the male mystery, to the
wonder and reverence of love, to the religious dimension. The experience is death to the relationship. In the Foreword to *Sons and
Lovers* Lawrence describes a similar relationship as blasphemous and
doomed to sterility:

> But if a man shall say "This woman is flesh of my flesh," let him see to
> it that he be not blaspheming the Father. For the woman is not flesh of
> his flesh by the bidding of the Word; but it is of the Father. And if he
> take a woman, saying in the arrogance of the Word, "The flesh of that
> woman is goodly," then he has said, "The flesh of that woman is goodly
> as a servant unto the Word, which is me," and so hath blasphemed the
> Father, by which he has his being, and she hath her being. And the flesh
> shall forsake these two, they shall be fabric of Word. And their race shall
> perish.[2]

Skrebensky marries another and goes to India, leaving Ursula pregnant
and ill with despair and self-doubt:

> She had been wrong, she had been arrogant and wicked, wanting that
> other thing, that fantastic freedom, that illusory, conceited fulfilment
> which she had imagined she could not have with Skrebensky. Who was
> she to be wanting some fantastic fulfilment in her life? . . . Suddenly
> she saw her mother in a just and true light. Her mother was simple and
> radically true. She had taken the life that was given. She had not, in her
> arrogant conceit, insisted on creating life to fit herself.

When Ursula becomes aware of her pregnancy, she is strongly
tempted to lapse from her struggle for self-effectuation, to take "the
life that was given." She writes a most moving letter to Skrebensky
asking him to take her back. She describes her former longings as crying for the moon:

[1] *Frieda Lawrence, The Memoirs and Correspondence,* ed. E. W. Tedlock, Heinemann (London), 1961, pp. 211–12.
[2] *The Letters of D. H. Lawrence,* ed. Aldous Huxley, Heinemann (London), 1932,
p. 98.

This letter she wrote, sentence by sentence, as if from her deepest, sincerest heart. She felt that now, now, she was at the depths of herself. This was her true self, forever. With this document she would appear before God at the Judgement Day.

If we had met this letter at the beginning of the book, we should have accepted Ursula's evaluation of it. It is true that Ursula's craving for self-satisfaction would have destroyed or driven off better men than Skrebensky, and that her attempts to create a life to fit herself are no more likely to be successful in the future than they have been. It is clearly the crisis of Ursula's life when an irrevocable decision must be made. And it seems that she has no alternative but to abandon her quest. But there is a crucial distinction to be made as subtle as that which defeats Peer Gynt—the distinction between being oneself and being oneself alone. Taking the given non-life and creating life to fit yourself are not the only alternatives.

Ursula, in response to some deep prompting, feels impelled to go for a walk in a downpour to escape the suffocation of the house. Her overwrought, almost hysterical state ("the seething rising to madness within her") manifests itself as a hyperconsciousness of elemental life and primitive forces looming, incarnate, around her. Bushes are "presences." The great veils of rain swinging across the landscape cause it to swim and fluctuate before her eyes.

It was very splendid, free and chaotic.

But only the chaos corresponds to her own inner experience, and so her response is fear:

She must beat her way back through all this fluctuation, back to stability and security. . . . Suddenly she knew there was something else.

At the narrative level it is only a group of horses, but Lawrence makes it very clear that they are also, and primarily, externalizations of her inner pressures and intimations:

She did not want to know they were there. . . . What was it that was drawing near her, what weight oppressing her heart? . . . [S]he went on, knowing things about them. She was aware of their breasts gripped, clenched narrow in a hold that never relaxed, she was aware of their red nostrils flaming with long endurance, and of their haunches, so rounded, so massive, pressing for ever till they went mad, running against the walls of time, and never bursting free. Their great haunches were smoothed and darkened with rain. But the darkness and wetness of rain could not put out the hard, urgent, massive fire that was locked within these flanks, never, never.

The early Brangwens had "mounted their horses and held life between the grip of their knees." But the life in these horses is violent and threatening, "clenched," "bursting," "mad," like Ursula's inner life. The Brangwen farmers had "harnessed the horses," incorporating the larger ever-potent life the horses stood for into their own temporal lives, entering the larger rhythms of life which include birth and death and thus transcending "the walls of time."

> Far back, far back in our dark soul the horse prances. He is a dominant symbol: he gives us lordship: he links us, the first palpable and throbbing link with the ruddy-glowing Almighty of potence: he is the beginning even of our godhead in the flesh. And as a symbol he roams the dark underworld meadows of the soul. He stamps and threshes in the dark fields of your soul and mine (*Apocalypse*, Ch. 10).

The horse as symbol of potency has been kept before us throughout the novel. Ursula had felt the body of the earth "stir its powerful flanks beneath her"; the darkness had been for her "passionate and breathing with immense unperceived heaving."

We hardly need the gloss provided by *Fantasia of the Unconscious* to realize that the horses represent "the great sensual male activity":

> A man has a persistent passionate fear-dream about horses. He suddenly finds himself among great, physical horses, which may suddenly go wild. Their great bodies surge madly round him, they rear above him, threatening to destroy him. At any minute he may be trampled down. . . . Examining the emotional reference we find that the feeling is sensual, there is a great impression of the powerful, almost beautiful physical bodies of the horses, the nearness, the rounded haunches, the rearing. . . .

This activity is normally repressed and seen as a menace to the soul's automatism—

> Whereas the greatest desire of the living spontaneous soul is that this very male sensual nature, represented as a menace, shall be actually accomplished in life.

Ursula's experience with the horses stands in polar contrast with her earlier dance of death with Skrebensky under a great white moon. That moon corresponds to "the fierce, white, cold passion in her heart":

> She was cold and hard and compact of brilliance as the moon itself, and beyond him as the moonlight was beyond him, never to be grasped or known.

It is a denial of relationship, of the other, blanching, sterile, reductive, confirming her in her solipsism and licence, her "cold liberty to be herself, to do entirely as she liked."

In the horses she must recognize what was not in Skrebensky to be recognized, "the triumphant, flaming, overweening heart of the intrinsic male," the potency of that life which is no part of her life, to which she must submit if she is ever to come into being.

The rhythms of the prose mime those of the horses, which in turn, as they approach, sheer off, circle, regroup, approach again, mime the rhythms of a mind struggling with its deepest problems and promptings, and moving, unconsciously, towards a resolution:

> The mind makes curious swoops and circles. It touches the point of pain or interest, then sweeps away again in a cycle, coils round and approaches again the point of pain or interest. There is a curious spiral rhythm, and the mind approaches again and again the point of concern, repeats itself, goes back, destroys the time-sequence entirely, so that time ceases to exist, as the mind stoops to the quarry, then leaves it without striking, soars, hovers, turns, swoops, stoops again, still does not strike, yet is nearer, nearer, reels away again, wheels off into air, even forgets, quite forgets, yet again turns, bends, circles slowly, swoops and stoops again, until at last there is the closing-in, and the clutch of a decision or a resolve (*Phoenix* 249–50).

Ursula cannot escape the extinction of her ego. Her fall from the oak tree is the breaking of all her connections with "the old, hard, barren form of bygone living" which must precede the issuing of the "naked, clear kernel" of herself, like an acorn bursting from its shell. It is a leap taken into the beyond, blindly, with no assurances. She is terribly ill, and loses her child. But the experience enables that which she is to come forth. Ursula glimpses something of the eternal and unchangeable that she is, that life is, that others may be:

> Who was she to have a man according to her own desire? It was not for her to create, but to recognize a man created by God. The man should come from the Infinite and she should hail him. She was glad she could not create her man. She was glad she had nothing to do with his creation. She was glad that this lay within the scope of that vaster power in which she rested at last.

Ursula's vision of the old world had been more and more as of a waste land, a purgatory peopled by those unfortunates who never were alive and those who, through cowardice, had made the great refusal. Industrialism, in particular, she had seen as "a pit-head surrounding the bottomless pit" (*Phoenix II* 385). But her own redemption seems to her to redeem the time, to constitute an assurance that all shall be well:

> She knew that the sordid people who crept hard-scaled and separate on the face of the world's corruption were living still, that the rainbow was arched in their blood and would quiver to life in their spirit. . . .

The urgent, massive fire locked within the flanks of the horses differs only in scale from the gleam of the nucleus under the microscope.

"The bluish, incandescent flash of the hoof-iron, large as a halo of
lightning round the knotted darkness of the flanks" is the same as the
flash of eyes and fangs and swords of angels she had glimpsed in the
darkness. The rainbow itself, a token of the covenant between God
and every living creature of all flesh, is a transformation of that fire
and that rain into being, relatedness, the crown of life.

The second and last sections of *The Crown* are virtually a commentary on the rainbow symbol. There the rainbow is an image of
the perfect balance of the great polar opposites which go to make up
life—sunshine and rain, air and water, light and dark, heaven and
earth:

> The wave of earth flung up in spray, a lark, a cloud of larks, against
> the white wave of the sun. The spray of earth and the foam of heaven
> are one, consummated, a rainbow mid-way, a song. The larks return to
> earth, the rays go back to heaven. But these are only the shuttles that
> weave the iris, the song, mid-way, in absoluteness, timelessness. (*Phoenix
> II* 375)

It is the meeting of the surrendered spirit and the creative unknown,
of aspiration and inspiration. This consummation or absoluteness
Lawrence calls being, or the fourth dimension, or the Holy Ghost.
Ursula's desire is that men should achieve it:

> One by one, in our consummation, we pass, a new star, into the galaxy
> that arches between the nightfall and the dawn, one by one, like the
> bushes in the desert, we take fire with God, and burn timelessly: and
> within the flame is heaven that has come to pass. . . . Every night new
> Heaven may ripple into being, every era a new Cycle of God may take
> place.

Towards the end of the novel such words as religion and God appear with great frequency. We must ask what, precisely, Lawrence
means by these words, whether he can be said to be writing, here,
within the Christian faith, or whether he is merely exploiting Christian terminology in an attempt to confer a spurious transcendence on
what is essentially a pantheistic position. In February 1915 Lawrence
wrote to Lady Ottoline Morrell:

> The strong soul must put off its connection with this society and go
> naked with its fellows, weaponless, armourless, without shield or spear,
> but only with naked hands and open eyes. Not self-sacrifice, but fulfil-
> ment, the flesh and the spirit in league together, not in arms against
> one another. And each man shall know that he is part of the greater
> body, each man shall submit that his own soul is not supreme even to
> himself . . . but that all souls of all things do but compose the body of
> God.[3]

[3] *The Collected Letters of D. H. Lawrence,* ed. Harry T. Moore, Heinemann
(London), 1962, Vol. I, p. 312.

At first glance the final clause would seem to be a classic statement
of pantheism; but it does not, in fact, exclude the possibility that
there might also be a soul of God not incarnate in "things." Life
itself is presented in the novel as something infinite and eternal, hardly
to be transcended. But whence, if God means Life, the benevolence
and purpose to which a man can submit in utter trust and nakedness?
Surely Lawrence was well aware of the objections to Wordsworthian
pantheism which Aldous Huxley exposed so trenchantly in *Wordsworth in the Tropics*? The ending of *St. Mawr* is the ultimate realisa-
tion of Huxley's point. But in *The Rainbow* there is no sense of the
senseless universe which nineteenth-century rationalism had discovered
and which had determined the form of Hardy's late novels.

The rainbow symbol reappears in *Kangaroo* as "a pledge of un-
broken faith, between the universe and the innermost." By 1922
Lawrence had stopped using the word God in more or less Christian
contexts and was beginning to talk about his "dark gods." But a "universe" which is capable of pledging faith seems to be in the sort of
personal and benevolent relationship with mankind which we associate with the Christian God. The symbol derives, of course, from
Genesis ix. 12–15, which is quoted in full in the novel and kept before us throughout:

> And God said: This is the token of the covenant which I make between
> me and you and every living creature that is with you, for perpetual
> generations; I do set my bow in the cloud, and it shall be a token of a
> covenant between me and the earth. And it shall come to pass, when I
> bring a cloud over the earth, that a bow shall be seen in the cloud; And
> I will remember my covenant, which is between me and you and every
> living creature of all flesh, and the waters shall no more become a flood
> to destroy all flesh.

The Rainbow is Lawrence's Isaiah, a reaffirmation of Noah's covenant
"from generation to generation."

The basic form of the novel, spread over three generations, is not
designed to allow Lawrence to present a social and cultural history
of English civilisation in the manner of George Eliot, nor even to
allow him to explore the psychological implications of heredity and
environment in the manner of Emily Brontë. He does both these
things, but incidentally. The structure shows how the Brangwens, beginning with the patriarch Tom, strive to keep this covenant while
the society around them is devoting more and more of its energy to
breaking it. To lose the relationship with God is to be in hell. But
the rainbow is "a sign that life will never be destroyed, or turn bad
altogether."

Lawrence uses the word "beyond" very frequently in *The Rainbow*.
At the beginning it seems to mean unknown areas of experience

within society (areas of which school and rectory and hall are tokens). In Ursula's adolescence it comes to signify also the darkness outside the area lit by the arc-lamp of man's civilised consciousness—both the elemental forces of nature and the subconscious forces in man. Thirdly, and in its most vivid realisations, it is the gleam at the centre of the living cell, the fire in the breasts of the horses, the rainbow arched in the blood of men, the God who is to be approached only by "a deeper immersion in existence" (Kierkegaard) and by "an openness to the holy, the sacred, in the unfathomable depths of even the most secular relationship" (Robinson):

> Who was she to have a man according to her own desire? It was not for her to create, but to recognise a man created by God. The man should come from the Infinite and she should hail him. She was glad she could not create her man. She was glad she had nothing to do with his creation. She was glad that this lay within the scope of that vaster power in which she rested at last.

What the Christian calls grace, Lawrence calls fulfilment.

In 1924 (*Books*) Lawrence wrote of his attitude to Christianity in terms which clearly refer to *The Rainbow*. It is a little-known passage worth quoting at length:

> During the Dark Ages . . . the flood of barbarism rose and covered Europe from end to end.
> But, bless your life, there was Noah in his Ark with the animals. There was young Christianity. There were the lonely fortified monasteries, like little arks floating and keeping the adventure afloat. There was no break in the great adventure in consciousness. Throughout the howlingest deluge, some few brave souls are steering the ark under the rainbow. . . .
> Once all men in the world lost their courage and their newness, the world would come to an end. . . .
> So we begin to see where we are. It's no good leaving everything to fate. Man is an adventurer, and he must never give up the adventure. . . .
> I know the greatness of Christianity: it is a past greatness. I know that, but for those early Christians, we should never have emerged from the chaos and hopeless disaster of the Dark Ages. If I had lived in the year 400, pray God, I should have been a true and passionate Christian. The adventurer.
> But now I live in 1924, and the Christian venture is done. The adventure is gone out of Christianity. We must start on a new venture towards God (*Phoenix* 733–4).

There is a sense in which Tom Brangwen, at the beginning of *The Rainbow,* did leave things to fate; and even Ursula, at the end, though she has made certain conscious rejections, is leaving her future fulfilment to fate. Rupert Birkin's "new venture towards God" is to be

of a radically different character, and largely accounts for the very
different formal characteristics of *Women in Love*. There is a sense
in *The Rainbow* that human purposes, when they are not mechanical
and deadly, subserve an evolutionary process which is God-given.
We feel that each generation, even when, exhausted, it lapses from the
adventure, is still held within a divine matrix. The creative process
is not complete within the individual life, but is carried forward
generation after generation, wave after wave, towards the shores of the
unknown. Ursula's wave is borne forwards on the residue of desire
from her parents and grandparents.

The rainbow is a symbol of this reality—"new heaven and earth,"
"a whole new world," "all that is to be." The novel is "the voyage of
discovery towards the real and eternal and unknown land." [4] It is not
romantic escapism, for the voyage is into and through the known, the
surface realities. This is the sense in which Lawrence defines poetry:

> The essential quality of poetry is that it makes a new effort of attention,
> and "discovers" a new world within the known world (*Phoenix* 255).

The creative imagination is here in close alliance with evolution, as
Lawrence understands it, in striving always towards greater and
greater distinctiveness and clarity:

> So on and on till we get to naked jelly, and from naked jelly to enclosed
> and separated jelly, from homogeneous tissue to organic tissue, on and
> on, from invertebrates to mammals, from mammals to man, from man to
> tribesman, from tribesman to me: and on and on, till, in the future,
> wonderful, distinct individuals, like angels, move about, each one being
> himself, perfect as a complete melody or a pure colour (*ibid.* 432).

Whether we move any further towards the angels or sink into a new
sort of savagery depends on the quality of our vision:

> The unspeakable inner chaos of which we are composed we call con-
> sciousness, and mind, and even civilisation. But it is, ultimately, chaos,
> lit up by visions, or not lit up by visions. Just as the rainbow may or
> may not light up the storm. And, like the rainbow the vision perisheth
> (*ibid.* 255).

[4] *Letters*, ed. Huxley, p. 240.

George H. Ford: *The Rainbow* and the Bible

Like the scene of Ursula's confronting the horses at the end of *The Rainbow,* the visit of Will and Anna Brangwen to Lincoln Cathedral is fitly regarded as a key scene in the novel. One of the many puzzles raised by this scene is why Lawrence chose to abandon the regular time sequence adhered to elsewhere in his chronicle. Chapter VI, "Anna Victrix," ends with an account of the static stage to which Will and Anna arrived some years *after* the cathedral incident. Apparently Lawrence wanted us to be aware throughout "The Cathedral" chapter of the way their dramatic conflict would be resolved.

A more significant feature of the presentation is that the visit to Lincoln is preceded by a visit to the vicarage of Baron Skrebensky, whose cultivated wife despises the "uncritical, unironical nature" of Will Brangwen so that his limitations are evident to his bride. Exposed to this household of light, the young Anna is reminded of "how different her own life might have been," and she realizes that through marriage she has been lapsing away from the individual pilgrimage towards critical self-knowledge on which she once felt she had been launched. Before she enters the cathedral, therefore, her guard is up, yet so powerful is the lure of darkness within the building that she has to struggle desperately to reassert her values, to laugh the walls and arches down so that light can get in. Specific phases of Christianity do come under her attack, but what she is really out to destroy is the religious sense itself.

For Will the ecstatic religious response he experiences within the dark interior is his "consummation," and every sentence of the lushly described ecstasy implies an analogy between religious union and sexual union—a blotting out of the mind and also of the whole world of time in which pilgrimages take place.

Lawrence's conception of what was, for him, the basic religious experience in the Edens of this world has nowhere been more finely rendered than here. How trite is the statement that a spire is a phallic

"The Rainbow and the Bible" (Editor's title). From Double Measure *by George H. Ford (New York: Holt, Rinehart and Winston, Inc., 1965), pp. 126–37. Copyright © 1965 by George H. Ford. Reprinted by permission of the publisher. The pages reprinted here are only part of the chapter entitled "The Rainbow as Bible."*

symbol and how boring to be told that a church is a womb or tomb symbol. Lawrence does not talk about symbols; he creates the experience. Moreover, to reinforce his analogy between religious consummation and sexual consummation he relies not only on the cathedral scene itself but upon our remembering another scene fifty pages earlier.

> Inside the room was a great steadiness, a core of living eternity. Only far outside, at the rim, went on the noise and the destruction. Here at the centre the great wheel was motionless, centred upon itself. Here was a poised, unflawed stillness that was beyond time, because it remained the same, inexhaustible, unchanging, unexhausted.

This passage describing the bedroom of the cottage in which Will and Anna spend their honeymoon uses exactly the same terms as are used to describe the cathedral. E. M. Forster would call such a repetition and appeal to the reader's memory an example of the novelist's use of musical techniques. In the present instance it is exceptionally effective:

> He was with her, as remote from the world as if the two of them were buried like a seed in darkness. . . . As they lay close together, complete and beyond the touch of time or change, it was as if they were at the very centre of all the slow wheeling of space and the rapid agitation of life, deep, deep inside them all, at the centre where there is utter radiance, and eternal being, and the silence absorbed in praise: the steady core of all movements, the unawakened sleep of all wakefulness. They found themselves there, and they lay still, in each other's arms; for their moment they were at the heart of eternity, whilst time roared far off, forever far off, towards the rim.

It is noteworthy too that the scene in the bedroom ends in exactly the same way as the scene in the cathedral. When the lovers count the strokes of the clock the darkness begins to dissipate, and when Anna insists upon seeing friends for a party the sanctuary of the bedroom is violated:

> He was anxious with a deep desire and anxiety that she should stay with him when they were in the timeless universe of free, perfect limbs and immortal breast. . . . But no, he could not keep her. She wanted the dead world again—she wanted to walk on the outside once more.

In the cathedral, the same impulse leads Anna to repudiate her husband's passionate need for remaining forever in spirit in the dark womb of the roofed building. "There was the sky outside," she reflects, "a space where stars were wheeling in freedom," and so she forces Will to regard the impish carved faces, mocking reminders, like the goblins that E. M. Forster detected in Beethoven's Fifth

Symphony, that the beautiful confined world of the marriage bed and of the cathedral is incomplete.

If this reading of the scene is an accurate one, we are still left with a puzzle to cope with—at least one puzzle. Is the cathedral with its arches to be identified with the arch of the rainbow? Throughout the novel, throughout Lawrence's writings in fact, rainbows are associated with the resolution of a stormy conflict between light and darkness, a token of hope for man's future.

Each of the three narratives into which the novel is divided concludes with a rainbow scene. Tom Brangwen's state of loneliness when he is disunited from his wife is compared vividly to his feeling "like a broken arch thrust sickeningly out from support." Later when his lonely state is relieved and man and wife come together in the familiar pattern of a "baptism to another life" their union is likened to the forming of a rainbow arch. The child Anna now "played between the pillar of fire and the pillar of cloud in confidence. . . . She was no longer called upon to uphold with her childish might the broken end of the arch. Her father and mother now met to the span of the heavens, and she, the child, was free to play in the space beneath, between."

When Anna is herself an adult, her own vision of the rainbow, as described at the end of Chapter VI, is as a token of hope. And Ursula, on the final page of the novel, after her vision of her own future and of mankind's future, discovers in the rainbow arch a resolution of her own stormy conflicts.

The arched cathedral, with its "jewelled gloom," can readily be identified with the traditional rainbow symbol, and Lawrence himself implies the comparison at several points. Yet he seems also to have realized that the identification as such can be misleading, and to have groped to suggest the differences between Will's response to the cathedral arch which shuts out the sky and Anna's response to the rainbow arch which is the sky. The dramatic conflict of forces in the cathedral scene concludes with both wife and husband "altered." The husband has discovered that the exclusively Dionysian darkness in which he reveled was half of life but no longer an absolute. The cathedrals, he realizes, do contain still, for him, "the dark mysterious world of reality," but he sees them now "as a world within a world . . . whereas before they had been as a world to him within a chaos . . . an absolute, within a meaningless confusion." [1]

[1] At a later stage in his marriage Will reverts to an "Absolute" again when he discovers that his wife's body is Absolute Beauty, the equivalent of the "absolute beauty of the round arch." Heretofore, we learn, he had preferred, like Ruskin, the pointed Gothic arches as emblematic of man's imperfection. The complexities introduced by this passage are excessive, for if we equate the rainbow arch with

Anna Brangwen too was "altered" by her exposure to what her young husband stood for:

> She was willing now to postpone all adventure into unknown realities. She had the child, her palpable and immediate future was the child [Ursula]. If her soul had found no utterance, her womb had.

What are we to understand by this *adventure into unknown realities?* In an earlier passage, Lawrence tries to convey the nature of this woman's search by analogies from the Bible. Anna, we learn, has stopped on Pisgah mount, from whence she can see the rainbow, a symbol of "the promise," but herself no longer a "traveller surging forward." And then, most strikingly, we encounter this analogy:

> The child she might hold up, she might toss the child forward into the furnace, the child might walk there, amid the burning coals . . . as the three witnesses walked with the angel in the fire.

To bring this subject blatantly and clumsily into the open, it can be said that *The Rainbow* is the story of the ancestry, birth, development, suffering, trials and triumphs of a prophet, or, more accurately, a prophetess, Ursula Brangwen, whose mission it will be to show the way out of a wilderness into a Promised Land. The comparison of Ursula to several great Biblical figures is exploited in a remarkable variety of ways. Her resemblance in the above passage to one of God's witnesses who can survive the test of fire is repeated, 250 pages later, on the night when she annihilates her lover, Skrebensky, in their final sexual encounter on the moonlit sand dunes:

> There was a great whiteness confronting her, the moon was *incandescent as a round furnace door,* out of which came the high *blast* of moonlight . . . a dazzling, terrifying glare of white light. . . . He felt himself *fusing* down to nothingness, like a bead that rapidly disappears in an incandescent flame [italics mine].

---

the classical arch a rich symbol becomes blurred and merely confusing. One can agree with Harry Levin's generalization in *The Power of Blackness* that the best symbols are indefinite in meaning, but we can draw the line when enrichment is simply misleading. The passage seems a kind of afterthought, but unfortunately it is one on which Mark Spilka leans hard in his discussion of *The Rainbow*. It misleads him, I suspect, to mix his arches with crosses. In his *Study of Thomas Hardy* (*Phoenix*, p. 454) Lawrence returns again to some assorted reflections on mediaeval cathedrals, but his most helpful discussion is an early letter contrasting Lincoln Cathedral with the commercial "temples" of London. The arches in London, he noted, "are round and complete; the domes high for the magnification of the voices," and the effect of these noisy buildings on the spectator is to make him feel cheerful and confident in the strength of human intelligence. The silence of the Gothic Cathedral, by contrast, is agitating, "mystical and wearying." Lincoln and Ely "set the soul a-quivering." (*Letters* [ed. Moore], I, 29.)

Only when we recall the Biblical parallel does this passage make its full impact or even make sense. Skrebensky is like the soldiers who conducted Shadrach, Meshach, and Abednego to the door of the fiery furnace, who were themselves consumed by flames that left God's witnesses unharmed.

If Ursula reminds us of Biblical prophets, what is Anna's role? Evidently she is cast as a forerunner, a Moses, a John, or even a Mary. The scene of her dancing naked during her pregnancy "to the unseen Creator who had chosen her," a scene that ranked as the most offensive in the book to the censors who banned *The Rainbow* in 1915, is actually a modern Magnificat.

Some readers will protest that such comparisons are offensive, and others that they are absurd or irrelevant. After all, Ursula Brangwen is an ordinary enough girl from a Nottinghamshire village, daughter of an inconsequential wood-carver and lace-designer, a girl who teaches school, attends college, and has an affair with an army officer.

Her mother's career is even more ordinary, and to imply that either woman's life has the significance we associate with the lives of the prophets is, such readers say, nonsense. The objection, though sound, can be met. On one dimension Lawrence is certainly presenting a prosy enough tale. His subject, as he said in a letter of 1914, was "woman becoming individual, self-responsible, taking her own initiative." [2] In this respect, *The Rainbow* (like *The Lost Girl* which he began to write at the same time) is concerned with a topic that used to be called Modern Woman, a topic that was being exploited, in a one-dimensional realistic and topical way in popular magazines and also by such writers as H. G. Wells and Arnold Bennett whose novels Lawrence had been reading and whose success he could not help but envy.

The Rainbow could have been another *Ann Veronica* (which Lawrence had read in 1910 and pronounced to be not very good). It is fortunately a great deal more, yet much of the book can compete with Wells or Bennett on their own terms. Ursula's experiences as a schoolteacher in the blackboard jungle of Ilkeston, for example, are largely of this topical and documentary dimension. The very title of the chapter devoted to these experiences, "The Man's World," suggests a problem novel of the Edwardian or Georgian era. On this level, then, what Lawrence calls Anna Brangwen's *adventure into unknown realities,* which she abandons, would mean simply female emancipation. Three generations of women are pictured as emerging from the bondage of the dark past into the light of the emancipated modern world.

---

[2] *Letters,* ed. Moore, I, 273.

The fact that the above phrase, *female emancipation,* falls with
a kind of dull thud and that *adventure into unknown realities* is not
offensive is in itself a promising sign. *The Rainbow* can convey impressively a sense of sixty years or more of English social history
from 1840 to 1905 let us say,[3] and yet convey even more impressively
a sense of timelessness.

The pilgrimages pursued by each generation in *The Rainbow* have
the effect of sagas, experiences that are recurrent in every age, in
which topicality is of minor consequence. How is this achieved? In
part it is because Lawrence had the good fortune or the good taste
to recognize that woman's suffrage, for example, was not likely to
prove a subject of lasting interest in a novel.

For Ursula "the liberty of woman meant something real and
deep. She felt that . . . she was not free." But "the automatic system
that contained the vote" is of little concern to her. Her search, instead,
is in the areas of "religion and living." Rather than upon politics,
or even the economic problem of competing with men for employ-
ment, Lawrence concentrates upon the personal and religious phases
of life, a man's or woman's fulfillment in relations with other men and
women, a topic most appropriate to the novelist. He also deals with
the characters' relations with God, a topic most appropriately dealt
with, if it is to be a literary subject, by the poet or poetic novelist.

The *adventure into unknown realities* is a timeless one partly because of the very imprecision of the phrase. What is it that Ursula,
as a "traveller," really wants? On the same night when she tests her
lover, Skrebensky, in the fiery furnace of the moonlight, we have this
characteristic exchange:

> She stood on the edge of the water, at the edge of the solid, flashing
> body of the sea, and the wave rushed over her feet.
> "I want to go," she cried, in a strong, dominant voice, "I want to
> go. . . ."
> "Where?" he asked.
> "I don't know."

The concluding admission, "I don't know," is an almost comically
lame one but it is not a period piece. Not being dependent on politi-

[3] There is some indication that Lawrence originally intended the action to end
about 1913 instead of 1905, but his use of the Boer War obliged him to push the
action back further. He seems to have had an eye out for possible anachronisms.
When Ursula, a late Victorian heroine in *The Rainbow,* rides through the country
in a "motor-car" (Chapter XI), it is evident that the experience is an unusual one
for the 1890's whereas in *Women in Love,* the motor-car is part of the landscape.
Even Birkin, unlike his creator, drives one. For an interesting analysis of how
Lawrence gains the effect of timelessness in individual scenes see Roger Sale's brief
essay "The Narrative Technique of *The Rainbow,*" *Modern Fiction Studies* V
(1959), pp. 29–38.

cal movements, the undefined yearning and dissatisfaction expressed by Lawrence's heroines in such scenes are represented as perennial human urges.

In addition to his focusing attention on personal relations and his minimizing of topicality, Lawrence achieves his effect of timeless interest in *The Rainbow* even more by his ambitious scheme of Biblical analogy. On one dimension, which *The Rainbow* shares with the novels of Wells and Bennett, Ursula is the ordinary village girl whose struggle to find herself in the modern world is representatively commonplace. On a second dimension, however, a dimension rarely represented at all in the novels of Wells and Bennett, this ordinary girl is likened to a prophet from the Bible whose life story is told as if it were of mythic or epic-scale significance.

The kind of reader, to whom I referred above, who finds the conception of Ursula as prophetess an absurd misreading will be well advised to devote himself to other novelists, for the Bible is not incidental decoration in *The Rainbow*; its mark is evident in the prose style, in the exalted pitch of scene, and in the underlying conception of the significance of each character's actions.[4]

Lawrence once described the Bible as "a great confused novel," and one is tempted, in the fashion of Oscar Wilde, to retort that *The Rainbow* is a great confused bible. The Bible, Lawrence adds, is not a book about God but about man alive: "Adam, Eve, Sarai, Abraham . . . Judas, Paul, Peter: what is it but man alive, from start to finish? . . . The Bible—but *all* the Bible—and Homer, and Shakespeare: these are the supreme old novels. These are all things to all men. Which means that in their wholeness they affect the whole man alive."[5]

We may be reminded of James Joyce's saying that Homer's *Odyssey* "embodies everything." Indeed there is considerable similarity between Joyce's use of Homeric parallels in *Ulysses* and Lawrence's use of Biblical parallels. Even though the apparent discrepancy between the large-scaled epic heroes and heroines of antiquity and their more ordinary modern-day equivalents is played up by Joyce for effects of comedy that are different from Lawrence's (especially when he is in Eastwood prophetic strain), the author of *Ulysses* is nevertheless using similar methods for similar ends. Both novelists, dissatisfied with the one-dimensional level of naturalistic fiction, create a second dimension

---

[4] On Lawrence's Protestantism, see J. H. Raleigh's "Victorian Morals and the Modern Novel," *Partisan Review*, XXV (1958), 241–64. For Lawrence's own comments, see *Apocalypse* and also his essay "Hymns in a Man's Life," in *Assorted Articles*, pp. 155–63. The Biblical influence on Lawrence's prose style has been analyzed by Frank Baldanza in *Modern Fiction Studies*, VII (1969), 106–14.

[5] *Phoenix*, pp. 535–36.

by suggesting, through parallels, that human experience is constant rather than totally chaotic.

The sense of order a reader derives from these repetitive spectacles can be ultimately reassuring and consolatory. . . . In *The Rainbow* what he is constantly trying to make us share is his sense that the Bible stories not only were but are. This goodly effort accords not only with the basic assumptions of his Protestant background, but with his conception of the function of literature.

Emma Bovary and her husband, Lawrence once noted, "are too insignificant to carry the full weight of Gustave Flaubert's sense of tragedy"[6]—an Aristotelian observation that is also applicable to Arthur Miller's *Death of a Salesman*. "The great tragic soul of Shakespeare," Lawrence adds, "borrows the bodies of kings and princes—not out of snobbism, but out of natural affinity."

In *The Rainbow* he cannot portray Anna Brangwen *as* a princess, but by surrounding her ordinary life with Biblical counterparts, he does portray her as *like* a princess.

Northrop Frye, in one of his several gallant attempts to slice out new categories from the traditional literary pie, suggests a scale of five fictional modes extending from myth (in which the hero or heroine is a divine being) through romance, epic, and the novel to the "ironic" mode in which the hero or heroine is inferior in power or intelligence to ourselves. In fifteen centuries, Frye notes, European fiction "has steadily moved its center of gravity down the list," with the ironic mode dominant in twentieth-century fiction[7]—in Bennett, we might say, or later in Kingsley Amis.

Lawrence's distinction, I am suggesting, is his mixture of modes. Beginning with Bennett, at the novelistic or ironic level, he moves on to endow his heroine with dimensions appropriate to myth, romance, and epic. *The Rainbow* thereby eludes classification not only in the traditional terms of novel-criticism but in Frye's more distinctive categories as well.

Joyce's use of Homer has received so much attention from scholars that readers can readily see the Odyssean shadows looming as counterparts behind every scene in his novel.

The Rainbow oddly enough has received less attention of this kind, perhaps because the old assumption dies hard that all educated readers will be thoroughly familiar with the minutiae of every page of the Bible. Lawrence himself, "soaked" in Biblical reading to the saturation point (as he says in *Apocalypse*), certainly makes such an assumption in his writings. His allusiveness takes a great deal for granted. In *Aaron's Rod*, for example, where he returns to some of

[6] *Phoenix*, p. 226.
[7] Northrop Frye, *Anatomy of Criticism* (Princeton, 1957), pp. 33–34.

the same Biblical parallels used in *The Rainbow,* there is the incident
of Lilly restoring the sick Aaron to health by rubbing his body with
camphorated oil.

For readers such as myself, more readily familiar with all the bi-
ographies of Lawrence than with certain passages of Exodus and
Leviticus and Numbers, this curious scene seemed significant only in
what it tells of an incident in Lawrence's own life, with homosexual
overtones, of which Middleton Murry has left an account.[8] Yet readers
as familiar with the Bible as Lawrence expected us to be will readily
recognize that allusion is being made to God's instructing Moses
(Exodus XXIX, 7, and XL, 15), "Then shalt thou take the anointing
oil, and pour it upon his head, and anoint him."

It is fascinating to speculate about Lawrence's preoccupations with
incidents having homosexual overtones, but we miss the core of
Aaron's Rod if we are sidetracked into overlooking the analogy to the
prophet consecrating his chief priest who will fail at times to follow
in his footsteps (Numbers XII and Exodus XXXII). Aaron Sisson's
vacillating attitudes towards the leadership of Lilly, the main subject of the novel, are forecast in the scene of his anointing and con-
secration.[9]

In a useful study of the ways in which the Bible has affected
twentieth-century novelists, *The Prophetic Voice in Modern Fiction*
(1959), William Mueller discusses novels by Joyce, Camus, Kafka,
Silone, Greene and Faulkner. It is curious that he says nothing of
Aaron's Rod and other novels by a writer who, more than any of
those named, reflects Biblical influences and correspondences on almost every page.

In *The Rainbow,* these correspondences occur in clusters. In many
instances they are not worked out rigidly. They serve simply to evoke
a general sense of resemblances. Thus Tom Brangwen is frequently
associated with Noah, as in his drunken death and the exposure of
his body to his children, but his death in a flood does not correspond
to the Bible story. What the novel is conveying to us effectively is a
general sense that the early Brangwens are patriarchal. The stories
about them which Ursula as a little girl hears in the Marsh bedroom
from Lydia, her grandmother, "became a sort of Bible to the child."

---

[8] J. M. Murry, *Reminiscences of D. H. Lawrence* (1936), p. 53.
[9] The lapse from the Biblical level into bathos is painfully illustrated in the
closing dialogue of *Aaron's Rod.* Of Lilly's advice to Aaron about what person he
should submit to ("Your soul will tell you") Anthony West comments witheringly
that this final exchange sounds like an anxious Victorian girl asking her Nannie:
"But how shall I know if it is Mr. Right?" "Your heart will tell you, dear, you
can't make a mistake when Mr. Right comes along." *D. H. Lawrence* (1950), p. 123.

Tom Brangwen is also, as I suggested earlier, associated with Eden, but as one who suffers at times from wondering what his role really is. At his daughter's wedding, he sees his life as a pilgrimage across a plain:

> He felt himself tiny, a little, upright figure on a plain circled round with the immense, roaring sky: he and his wife, two little, upright figures walking across this plain, whilst the heavens shimmered and roared about them.

In this figure we have the principal link between *The Rainbow* and the Bible as a whole. The movement of each generation, even for those who pause in the journey across the plain, is away from Eden towards the promised land and eventually towards the kind of far-reaching changes in man's state that are forecast in the Apocalyptic vision. Of such changes, as the last paragraph of the novel indicates with its rainbow symbol, Ursula Brangwen is to bear witness.

In *The Plumed Serpent* Kate actually becomes a priestess (admittedly a somewhat reluctant one) of a new cult, a situation that strained Lawrence's fictional resources to the breaking point. In *The Rainbow* Ursula's role is conveyed, instead, by an analogy which achieves the dimension desired without incongruity because of the very vagueness of her mission. The heightening gained by the effective use of the mythic method functions in this novel for prophecy as well as for history and fiction.

William Walsh: The Childhood of Ursula

Part of the rich and varied intention of *The Rainbow* is to render the life of the too intensely loved, the over-possessed child. A deep, not fully conscious disharmony between her parents is a predisposing cause of Ursula's relationship with her father. It makes itself felt again immediately the child is born. "It was a girl. The second of silence on her face when they said so showed him she was disappointed. And a great blazing passion of resentment and protest sprang up in his heart. In that moment he claimed the child." The intemperance of Will Brangwen's response—his resentment and his angry "claim"—is more than a passing irritation with Anna's remark or fury at an imagined slight on himself. It derives also from a profound inadequacy in himself.

"The Childhood of Ursula" (Editor's title). From The Use of Imagination *by William Walsh (London: Chatto and Windus Ltd., 1959), pp. 163–74. Reprinted by permission of the author and the publisher. The pages reprinted here are only part of the chapter entitled "The Writer and the Child."*

He was aware of some limit to himself, of something unformed in his way of being, of some buds which were not ripe in him, some folded centres of darkness which would never develop and unfold whilst he was alive in the body. He was unready for fulfilment. Something undeveloped in him limited him, there was a darkness in him which he *could* not unfold, which would never unfold in him.

From the first a very special relationship existed between Ursula and her young father, a strong and intense intimacy that he hardly dared acknowledge. When the child cried in the night, he was shaken intolerably: it seemed to him that the crying came from "the awful, obliterated sources which were the origin of his living tissue." He was moved by the baby's strange, new beauty. "He saw the lovely, creamy, cool little ear of the baby, a bit of dark hair, rubbed to a bronze floss, like bronze-dust." And the child, too, was as stirred by his presence. Its eyes lit up and dilated when he was by. "It knew its mother better, it wanted its mother more. But the brightest, sharpest little ecstasy was for the father." When he saw "the tiny living thing rolling naked in the mother's lap . . . in a world of hard surfaces and varying altitudes . . . vulnerable and naked at every point," he saw it as an image, a living analogy with his own vulnerability, "the terror of being so utterly delivered over, helpless at every point."

Persistently, one idea threads its way in and out of these pages recording the beginnings of Ursula's life. It is the idea of possession, of the father's ownership of the child. His original "claim" issues from this sense of possession, and insistently the same note is repeated. "He waited for the child to become his. . . . It was his own. . . . So that the father had the elder baby. . . . She was a piece of light that really belonged to him, that played within his darkness." The ownership implicit in these phrases is not that involved in the possession of an object outside and at some distance from the possessor. It is much closer to that mysterious and uneasy proprietorship which a person has over himself. Theoretically, the father recognises that the child has a life different from his own, but that recognition is absorbed in his passion of possession. "It had a separate being, but it was his own child. His flesh and blood vibrated to it." The root of this almost desperate sense of possession is the father's deep uncertainty about himself and his need therefore to be constantly reassured. The child, he feels, in its vivid response to him, is a kind of proof of his own being. "As the newly-opened, newly-dawned eyes looked at him, he wanted them to perceive him, to recognise him. Then he was verified."

In this too charged, overstrained atmosphere Ursula's life begins. Probably not since Wordsworth has a writer conveyed with such essential justice the first stirrings of consciousness, the first movements

of the body. Some of the subtlety of Lawrence's portrayal is to be attributed to his having been brought up himself in similar circumstances with his mother filling the role of Ursula's father; more to his
extraordinary sense of otherness, his capacity to enter into wholly different natures; but most is to be attributed to his genius for transmut-
ing his experience and ordering his capacities so as to make them
both serve with delicate rightness the purposes of his art. And his
art is above all an art which uses poetic means to reveal the universal
human substance, the permanent, impersonal energy which in other
novelists we find almost dissolved in "character" or encrusted with
accidents. How exactly and how convincingly, for example, Lawrence
in the following passage catches that generic motion of childhood,
the strange drifting movement of a young child hurrying, when it
seems hardly tethered to the ground and when, with an odd mixture
of confidence and uncertainty, it performs miracles of balance and ac-
commodation.

> At evening, towards six o'clock, Anna very often went across the lane
> to the stile, lifted Ursula over into the field, with a: "Go and meet
> Daddy." Then Brangwen, coming up the steep round of the hill, would
> see before him on the brow of the path a tiny, tottering, wind-blown
> little mite with a dark head, who, as soon as she saw him, would come
> running in tiny, wild, windmill fashion, lifting her arms up and down
> to him, down the steep hill. His heart leapt up, he ran his fastest to her,
> to catch her, because he knew she would fall. She came fluttering on,
> wildly, with her little limbs flying. And he was glad when he caught her
> up in his arms.

As convincing, equally exact, and profound in a way that recalls
Wordsworth's subterranean explorations of the mind, is Lawrence's
record of the beginnings of the child's thought. At first Ursula's life
is just an aggregation of incidents, each sliding unemphatically into
the next; to the child an event is neither provoked by the one before
nor productive of the one after. In this world, bare of shadows and
suggestiveness, the brightness and prominence of reality belong only
to the immediate and the explicit.

> The child ran about absorbed in life, quiet, full of amusement. She
> did not notice things, nor changes nor alterations. One day she would
> find daisies in the grass, another day apple-blossoms would be sprinkled
> white on the ground, and she would run among it, for pleasure because
> it was there. Yet again birds would be pecking at the cherries, her father
> would throw cherries down from the tree all around her on the garden.
> Then the fields were full of hay.

The child's consciousness, which is partial and successive, does not include a sense of the past or the future. It has to be discovered, and

the provocation to learn it is love. Affection is the seed of time. It is love—intensifying the delight in the present and correspondingly bringing discomfort in absence—which introduces an element of permanence into the child's experience, and the first faint notion of time into its mind.

> She did not remember what had been nor what would be, the outside things were there each day. She was always herself, the world outside was accidental. . . . Only her father occupied any permanent position in the childish consciousness. When he came back she remembered vaguely how he had gone away, when he went away she knew vaguely that she must wait for his coming back. Whereas her mother, returning from an outing, merely became present, there was no reason for connecting her with some previous departure.

The love between father and daughter is the first organising influence in Ursula's mental life, shaping even those essential ideas of time, permanence and change, the self and what lies outside it, which henceforth order all human thoughts and render all experience intelligible. But there is something strained and distorted in the father's love—it is too narrow, too possessive, too personal. It is the kind of love which consumes its object, which cannot keep its distance or allow its object any degree of autonomy. The father's love springs from some incoherence in his own nature, an absence of serenity or self-acceptance; it is a projection of his own need, his own tension and inadequacy. And so intricately is the child involved with him that it is impossible for him to make the painful and wrenching effort necessary for regarding Ursula as another being, separate, autonomous and sufficient. In Will, Lawrence presents us with an extreme example of that failure of nerve and of that want of clarity of being present in every parent for whom the umbilical cord is never cut. This quality in the father's love conditions the affection Ursula returns to him. His is dependent, hers protective, a strange reversal of natural roles. "When he was disagreeable, the child echoed to the crying of some need in him, and she responded blindly. Her heart followed him as if he had some tie with her, and some love which he could not deliver. Her heart followed him persistently, in its love." To base one's life, like Will Brangwen, on the support and accord of a young child is to put an intolerable strain on the child. The relaxed rhythm of childhood is shattered, and the child, like Ursula, is jerked too early into a too sharpened awareness. As in a premature birth, she is pulled from a mindless tranquillity towards a too urgent, a too personal concern.

> Her father was the dawn wherein her consciousness woke up. But for him, she might have gone on like the other children, Gudrun and

Theresa and Catherine, one with the flowers and insects and playthings, having no existence apart from the concrete object of her attention. But her father came too near to her. The clasp of his hands and the power of his breast woke her up almost in pain from the transient unconsciousness of childhood. Wide-eyed, unseeing, she was awake before she knew how to see.

Will Brangwen's love for his daughter is a narrow and therefore narrowing love. It has an exclusive character which inspires in the child a corresponding jealousy and resentment for anyone outside the magic alliance who attempts to break into it. In particular, Ursula's resentment is directed against her mother's influence and authority. And this is so even when her mother intervenes in her defence against the sporadic, senseless acts of cruelty which her father, in a kind of angry impotence, commits against her. There are several examples of these negative, destructive impulses into which Will's frantic unbalanced love seems to drive him almost against his will. There is, for example, the violence with which he attacks Ursula when in her play about the church she disturbs the hymnbooks and cushions, or again there is the sadistic cruelty with which he terrifies and sickens the child by driving her unbearably high on the swing-boat at the fair. The demands of her father's love come out of his own weakness. So exigent a love diminishes and damages its object, which can never feel adequate to the immense claims made upon it. Ursula is overwhelmed by her vast, vaguely grasped responsibility towards her father. She is filled with "the painful, terrified helplessness of childhood."

> Still she set towards him like a quivering needle. All her life was directed by her awareness of him, her wakefulness to his being. . . . But there was the dim, childish sense of her own smallness and inadequacy, a fatal sense of worthlessness. She could not do anything, she was not enough. . . . This knowledge deadened her from the first.

"It deadened her." This image of mortification is the one through which Lawrence expresses his deepest judgment on Will's relationship with Ursula. Love is the generator and protector of life. But Will's is a killing love. It hardens the child. It puts a blight, a frost on her. It brings disillusion, "something cold and isolating." The scene in which Lawrence's judgment is most powerfully and dramatically realised is that in which Ursula is helping her father to plant potatoes in his garden. It is beautifully appropriate that the occasion for the scene should be a collision between what is most intensely real and important to the child—the universe of play and fancy—and what is to her the mystery of the grown-up power to work deliberately, something the child dreads because it is impossible for her and because it makes her father a stranger to her. Ursula was delighted and excited when Will asked her to help him. " 'Ay,' he said, 'you can put some taters in for me. Look—like that—these little sprits standing up—so much apart, you see.' And stooping down he quickly, surely placed the spritted potatoes in the soft grip, where they rested separate and pathetic on the heavy cold earth." But the operation was too difficult, too serious and too long for the child. She fumbles and be-becomes afraid and overcome by her responsibility. Her father works on confidently, ignoring her as she stands "helplessly stranded on his world." When he came by he said to her, " 'You didn't help me much.' The child looked at him dumbly. Already her heart was heavy because of her own disappointment. Her mouth was dumb and pathetic. But he did not notice. He went his way."

Then the next day he smashes even more destructively into her sensitive child's world. "He turns on her, shouting, 'Who's been tramplin' an' dancin' across where I've just sowed seed? I know it's you, nuisance! Can you find nowhere else to walk, but just over my seed-beds? But it's like you, that is—no heed but to follow your own greedy nose.' " The vulnerable child is shocked. "She stood dazzled with pain and shame and unreality. Her soul, her consciousness seemed to die away. She became shut off and senseless, a little fixed creature whose soul had gone hard and unresponsive. The sense of her own unreality hardened her like a frost. She cared no longer." And when, inflamed by her indifference, he threatens to strike her, "the child did not alter in the least. The look of indifference, com-plete glancing indifference, as if nothing but herself existed to her, remained fixed. Yet far away in her the sobs were tearing her soul. And when he had gone, she would go and creep under the parlour sofa, and lie clinched in the silent, hidden misery of childhood."

It takes a very great writer to make us feel, as we do here, beneath the simple surface of a familiar domestic event, like a father's anger with his child because her play interfered with his work, the vibra-tions of a deep and complex human disaster. And disastrous is not too extravagant a way to describe the effect of these experiences with her father on Ursula's life. As well as the child's natural mortification at her father's brutality, she suffers another kind of mortification—"a deadening of the soul"—more permanent and injurious in its conse-quences. After such bitterness the child's instinctive response is to blot out the memory of what has happened

so that the pain and the insult should not be real. She asserted herself only. There was now nothing in the world but her own self. So very soon she came to believe in the outward malevolence that was against her. And very early she learned that even her adored father was part of this malevolence. And very early she learned to harden her soul in re-

sistance and denial of all that was outside her, harden herself upon her
own being.

A healthy love helps the child to accept the order and justice of the
world and to recognise the fundamental goodness and sanity of life itself. But one like Will's communicates its distortion to the child's very
sensibility so that it sees a disturbed and malicious world from
which it must flee into itself. Nor is this all. A child can tolerate a
malevolent world only by denying its reality, and so like Ursula it
becomes convinced of, and tortured by, the illusion and trickery of
everything beyond its own identity.

> But she was always tormented by the unreality of outside things. The
> earth was to walk on. Why must she avoid a certain patch, just because
> it was called a seed-bed? It was the earth to walk on. This was her instinc-
> tive assumption. And when he bullied her, she became hard, cut herself
> off from all connection, lived in the little separate world of her own
> violent will.

As she grew older the relationship between Ursula and her father
did not cease. But it was tense and anxious, always straining to break.
Her father remained for Ursula "a centre of magic and fascination,"
so that "she seemed to run in the shadow of some dark potent secret
of which she would not, of whose existence even she dared not become
conscious, it cast such a spell over her, and so darkened her mind."
And yet the child was continually striving for her own separate
identity, "always relapsing on her own violent will into her own
separate world of herself." "When she returned to her love for her
father, the seed of mistrust and defiance burned unquenched, though
covered up far from sight. She no longer belonged to him unquestioned. Slowly, slowly, the fire of mistrust and defiance burned in
her. . . ." But they were never wholly separated, never cleanly broken
apart into their own different identities, which would have been the
condition of a true and sound relationship. "There was this curious
taunting intimacy between them." With it persisted Ursula's sense of
the world, whether the world of home or of school or of neighbours
or of authority, as illusory and menacing.

> There was always this menace against her. This strange sense of cruelty
> and ugliness always imminent, ready to seize hold upon her, this feeling
> of the grudging power of the mob lying in wait for her, who was the
> exception, formed one of the deepest influences of her life. Wherever
> she was, at school, among friends, in the street, in the train, she instinc-
> tively abated herself, made herself smaller, feigned to be less than she
> was, for fear that her undiscovered self should be seen, pounced upon,
> attacked by brutish resentment of the commonplace, the average Self.

There are three influences on Ursula which qualify her father's, which to some degree mitigate the harm to the child of Will's excessive, too personal attachment, and which help her "to move out of the intricately woven illusion of her life." They are her grandmother, the Grammar School and religion. Each of them represents an order, larger and more enduring, calmer and wiser than the nervous, stormy life at home. Each accords a measure of dignity and a recognition of her own self to the young girl. Each of them helps to satisfy her craving "for some spirituality and stateliness." The power and the delicacy with which Lawrence exhibits the exact character of each of these influences must be one of the great fictional and poetic achievements of modern literature.

Lydia Brangwen had retired from the stress and violence and the interested passion of the young. "She wanted at last her own innocence and peace." At her grandmother's Ursula found gentleness, understanding and a completely disinterested affection. "The little girl and the musing fragile woman of sixty seemed to understand the same language. . . . So that for the eldest child the peace of her grandmother's bedroom was exquisite. Here Ursula came as to a hushed, paradisal land, here her own existence became simple and exquisite to her as if she were a flower." The sense of restraint and civilised order is implicit in each tiny detail of Ursula's meetings with her grandmother. "Ursula had a special green and gold cup kept for herself at the house. There was thin bread and butter, and cress for tea. It was all special and wonderful. She ate very daintily, with little fastidious bites." That the civilisation—"the spirituality and stateliness"—which she loved in her grandmother was ancient and rooted and remote was a marvellous thing to the child. Her heart beat as she listened to her grandmother's stories of the family and its origins. "She could not understand, but she seemed to feel far-off things. It gave her a deep, joyous thrill to know she hailed from far-off Poland, and that dark-bearded impressive man." It was to her grandmother that Ursula addressed "her deepest childish questions."

> "But when I am grown up, will somebody love me?"
> "Yes, some man will love you, child, because it's your nature. And I hope it will be somebody who will love you for what you are, and not for what he wants of you."
> She clung to her grandmother. Here was peace and security. Here, from her grandmother's peaceful room, the door opened on to the greater space, the past, which was so big that all it contained seemed tiny; loves and births and deaths, tiny units and features within a vast horizon. That was a great relief to know the tiny importances of the individual, within the great past.

If her grandmother brings Ursula into the presence of an ancient civilisation and the comfort of the past, the Grammar School at Not-

tingham to which she goes at the age of twelve gives Ursula a great
liberation in the present. Ursula's life at home as the eldest of a large
family was onerous and responsible. The little ones depended on her,
hunted her out when she wished to be alone and swept her along in
"a storm of movement" from which there was no escape. "She hated
so much being in charge," and was continually fretted by her responsibility to the others. The small house filled with the press and
swirl of babies and young children became a nightmare to her. "When
she saw, later, a Rubens picture with storms of naked babies and
found this was called 'Fecundity,' she shuddered and the word became
abhorrent to her. She knew as a child what it was to live amid storms
of babies, in the heat and swelter of fecundity." From all this the
Grammar School afforded her a retreat, a space to collect herself in.
It also rescued her from the village school with its "meagre teachers"
and the niggardly and begrudging companionship of the village children. Above all it introduced her to the life of learning and intelligence. Lawrence brilliantly communicates the joy and excitement
and the deep sense of liberation of the intelligent child's first discovery of the forms of educated thought.

> She was happy. Up here, in the Grammar School, she fancied the air
> was finer, beyond the factory smoke. She wanted to learn Latin and
> Greek and French and mathematics. She trembled like a postulant when
> she wrote the Greek alphabet for the first time. She was upon another
> hill-slope, whose summit she had not scaled. There was always the mar-
> vellous eagerness in her heart, to climb and to see beyond. A Latin
> verb was virgin soil to her: she sniffed a new odour in it; it meant
> something, though she did not know what it meant. But she gathered
> it up: it was significant. When she knew that:
>
> $$x^2 - y^2 = (x + y) \ (x - y)$$
>
> then she felt that she had grasped something, that she was liberated
> into an intoxicating air, rare and unconditioned. And she was very glad
> as she wrote her French exercise:
>
> "J'ai donné le pain à mon petit frère."
>
> In all these things there was the sound of a bugle to her heart, ex-
> hilarating, summoning her to perfect places.

The third of these influences on Ursula was religion. The special
character of Brangwen Christianity was its appeal to the absolute,
the insistence on the otherness of God. It is as though the intimacy
of their family relationships needed to be balanced by the remoteness
of the Almighty. They—and most of all Ursula—had no patience with
a familiar, domestic piety. "They wanted the sense of the eternal
and immortal, not a list of rules for everyday conduct. . . . It was
the vulgar mind which would allow nothing extra-human, nothing
beyond itself to exist. . . . But Ursula was all for the absolute. . . .

To her Jesus was another world, He was not of this world." The centre of their religious life was Christmas, and to a lesser degree, like a diminishing echo, Sunday. At Christmas they felt the reality of the absolute, and its closeness and power. "Everywhere was a sense of mystery and rousedness. Everyone was preparing for something." Then they felt the ecstasy, even if, as traditional religion declined, "it was faint and inadequate. The cycle of creation still wheeled in the Church year. After Christmas, the ecstasy slowly sank and changed. Sunday followed Sunday, trailing a fine movement, a finely developed transformation over the heart of the family." It is this great tradition, the richness and spirituality of which the novel superbly reconstructs, that dignifies and enlarges the lives of the children. Its more than temporal rhythms relax the tension of lives too frantically engrossed with the immediate. Its impersonal harmony incorporates into itself the stresses and muddle of the merely personal life.

> So the children lived the year of christianity, the epic of the soul of mankind. Year by year the inner, unknown drama went on in them, their hearts were born and came to fulness, suffered on the cross, gave up the ghost, and rose again to unnumbered days, untired, having at least this rhythm of eternity in a ragged, inconsequential life.

Laurence Lerner: Lawrence's "Carbon"

It is not impossible for a novelist to learn something from experts and then go back and rediscover it as a version of experience: but it must be very difficult indeed. Lawrence is a writer who tried to work out his own psychology, but he did so at a time when there were technical psychologies about him. He did not have to discover the unconscious: the term was given to him, from outside. . . . [T]his was not altogether an advantage to him.

Compare, for instance, these two passages:

> It is like a lovely, suave, fluid, *creative* electricity that flows in a circuit between the great nerve-centres in mother and child. The electricity of the universe is a sundering force. But this lovely polarised vitalism is creative. It passes in a circuit between the two poles of the passional unconscious in the two now separated beings. It establishes in each that first primal consciousness which is the sacred, all-containing head-stream of all our consciousness.[1]

"Lawrence's 'Carbon.' " From The Truthtellers *by Laurence Lerner (London: Chatto and Windus Ltd.; New York: Schocken Books, Inc., 1967), pp. 78–82. Copyright © 1967 by Laurence Lerner. Reprinted by permission of the author and the publishers.*

[1] *Psycho-analysis and the Unconscious,* § 3

From the first the baby stirred in the young father a deep, strong emotion he dared scarcely acknowledge, it was so strong and came out of
the dark of him. When he heard the child cry, a terror possessed him,
because of the answering echo from the unfathomed distances in himself.
Must he know in himself such distances, perilous and imminent? [2]

The first is Lawrence's account of mother-love, from a theoretical
work; the second his expression of father-love, from a novel. Because
it is Lawrence, the style and approach are barely different, but what
difference there is is most revealing. What has it helped the first
passage that Lawrence can use the terms "conscious" and "unconscious"? It has not lessened the dependence on metaphor, almost on
invocation; nor has it disciplined the thought. It is not clear how
seriously we are to take "establishes" (similar, that, to Freud's too-
ready belief that he knows which way causation works); and I can at-
tach little meaning to "the electricity of the universe is a sundering
force."

Now the second passage is not only much more compelling, the
whole paragraph having a rhythmic shape and the ring of genuine
emotion: it is also written with more clarity. The unfathomed distances are clearer to us than the "passional unconscious": there is
no pretence in this passage of greater precision than the writer can
command. Instead of the pretentious vocabulary of the "lovely po-
larised vitalism," there is a willingness to say only what he knows,
rendering the emotion even if the psychology is guesswork.

Lawrence did not go beneath the surface of consciousness as
thoughtfully as George Eliot, but he went further, and more often.
She may describe the structure of carbon with more care, but there
is far more of it in his books than in hers. In this, he is a modern:
just as [her] gropings . . . make her, typical Victorian as she is, a
proto-modern.

What makes a writer modern need not be what makes him good;
and it is not easy to be sure how far Lawrence's interest in carbon
is a source of strength to his novels, and how far of weakness. A
good test case is the superb thirteenth chapter of *The Rainbow*, the
account of Ursula's spell of teaching in a slum school. The scene
I want to discuss is . . . too long to quote, and I must fob off the
reader with a summary and a plea that he turn it up. It is the scene
in which Mr Harby, the Headmaster, passes her classroom and hears
the jeering note in the voices of the boys as (against the rules) they
call out their answers.

At that moment Mr Harby was passing.
    "Stand up, Hill!" he called, in a big voice.

[2] *The Rainbow*, ch. 8

Everybody started. Ursula watched the boy. He was evidently poor, and rather cunning. A stiff bit of hair stood straight off his forehead, and the rest fitted close to his meagre head. He was pale and colourless.

"Who told you to call out?" thundered Mr Harby.

"Please sir, I was answering," he replied, with the same humble insolence.

"Go to my desk."

The boy set off down the room, the big black jacket hanging in dejected folds about him, his thin legs, rather knocked at the knees, going already with the pauper's crawl, his feet in their big boots scarcely lifted. Ursula watched him in his crawling, slinking progress down the room. He was one of *her* boys!

Mr Harby then stays for a few minutes to examine the class.

"What is your composition about?" asked the Headmaster. Every hand shot up. "The—" stuttered some voice in its eagerness to answer.

"I wouldn't advise you to call out," said Mr Harby. He would have a pleasant voice, full and musical, but for the detestable menace that always tailed in it. He stood unmoved, his eyes twinkling under his bushy black eyebrows, watching the class. There was something fascinating in him, as he stood, and again she wanted to scream. She was all jarred, she did not know what she felt.

"Well, Alice?" he said.

"The rabbit," piped a girl's voice.

"A very easy subject for Standard Five." [3]

Ursula, stuck among the back forms, can do nothing but listen. She finds herself disliking Mr Harby for his bullying, the aggressive imposing of his cheap authority; yet at the same time she finds him an attractive man, "with strength and male power and a certain blind, native beauty." While she is reflecting on this contradiction—puzzled, humiliated, resentful—Mr Harby goes to his desk and beats Hill, who comes "crawling back, blubbering piteously." His misery does not last as long as her shame; and in the end the lesson returns to normal—or the nearest Ursula can ever come to normal.

This is one of Lawrence's great scenes, unforgettably true and powerful. It is the work of someone who has seen and heard with vivid accuracy, and whose details are arresting in their realism—the "big voice" with which Mr Harby calls out, the boy's "cunning, cynical reserve," and above all (an objective image for Ursula's whole complex reaction of shame, dislike and pity) the superbly rendered walk, the "pauper's crawl" with which Hill goes to Mr Harby's desk, leaving Ursula doubly ashamed, that Hill should represent her before Mr Harby, and that she should have got Hill into trouble. Lawrence can catch an overtone in a phrase: "a very easy

[3] *The Rainbow,* ch. 13

subject for Standard Five" captures exactly the tone in which Mr
Harby would rebuke Ursula under the guise of rebuking her class.
Lawrence is writing here with the steady eye and keen observation of
one of the great realists—Zola, say, or Arnold Bennett.

Yet Bennett could not have written this scene. Perhaps there is no
detail, in the parts I have quoted, altogether out of the range of
Bennett's realism, though he seldom scores so many bullseyes together;
but the long paragraph analysing Ursula's feelings towards Mr Harby
is quite foreign to the world of *The Old Wives' Tale* and *Riceyman
Steps*. In part, it is a reflection on the pointlessness of authority:

> He had a decent, powerful, rude soul. What did he care about the com-
> position on "The Rabbit"? Yet his will kept him there before the class,
> threshing the trivial subject. It was habit with him now, to be so little
> and vulgar, out of place. She saw the shamefulness of his position, felt
> the fettered wickedness in him which would blaze out into evil rage
> in the long run, so that he was like a persistent, strong creature tethered.
> It was really intolerable. The jarring was torture to her.[4]

There is a great deal more like this, in a paragraph almost as
long as the rest of the scene. It is an exploring of the edge of consciousness. Ursula is conscious of most (perhaps not quite all) of this
train of thought; but the part of Mr Harby's nature she is pondering
is largely unconscious. She is distressed above all by his "blind, dogged,
wholesale, will."

"Will" is one of the commonest and most puzzling of Lawrence's
psychological terms. It usually means an intense determination to
act that is not based on the "candle flame, forever upright and flow-
ing" which represents his ideal of the whole man. It is always a
derogatory term. The result of this violence of will in Mr Harby is
"the fettered wickedness in him which would blaze out into evil rage
in the long run." Here we are beyond the personality of Mr Harby,
on the edge of meeting something very like an account of repression.
This is not diamond, but carbon.

It is Lawrence's interest in the general (including the unconscious)
operation of psychic forces ("Diamond, what! This is carbon") that
takes him beyond the range of a realist like Bennett. Lawrence is
able to render the surface of this scene with such superb truth because
he is sensitive to what goes on beneath the surface. We praise Bennett
for his honesty: for the human warmth without idealisation that can
portray (say) the relationship between Violet and Elsie is *Riceyman
Steps*. But Lawrence is so much more honest—he gets in so much more
of the irritations, the exact intonations of malice, shame or love—
that after reading him we can never feel quite the same about Bennett.

---

[4] Ibid., ch. 13

Bennett seems to touch us on the quick when he writes about domestic tensions and resentment; but compared to Lawrence he is always slightly reserved.

And so we can say that if Lawrence had not been able to write that exploring paragraph in which Ursula analyses Mr Harby, he would not have been able to employ that hypersensitive eye and ear, and would not have caught the realistic details of speech and crawl so vividly: by transcending realism, he becomes greater than the realists at their own method. This is true: but it is also true that the long paragraph of analysis is a flaw. Many readers must wish it away; almost all readers must wish it shorter. Only by quoting it all can one convey the repetitiveness, the wearisome, almost pedantic repetitiveness, that dilutes and hinders its impact; and there are details which can be seen in quotation. How slovenly, for instance, is the adjective "wholesale," when Lawrence writes of Mr Harby's "blind, dogged, wholesale will." And after the powerful sentence about the "fettered wickedness in him," Lawrence descends with shocking insensitivity to "It was really intolerable." There was not a single false note in the dramatic rendering of the scene itself, but Lawrence loses all that perfect control when he turns to deal with what lies beneath the surface.

We can see the same thing on a larger scale by comparing *The Old Wives' Tale* with *The Lost Girl*. Lawrence may have written his novel in imitation of Bennett—certainly there can be no doubt of the influence. The first third or so of *The Lost Girl* is as vivid and powerful as Bennett (it seems to me the one Lawrence novel that his admirers underrate), and its occasional sense of the depths that lurk beneath what is observed make it in many ways greater; but there is nothing in *The Old Wives' Tale* as tedious as the Natcha-Kee Tawaras, nor any character as pretentiously created as Cicio.

Lawrence's description of himself as "religious," we may then conclude, though it is misleading, points to something of great importance in his work, perhaps the most important quality of all, his interest in carbon. It is this that makes him modern, and it is this that makes him great; but this is also the source of his stridency, tediousness and vagueness.

PART FOUR

The Making of The Rainbow

The Marble and the Statue

by Mark Kinkead-Weekes

. . . you know that the perfect statue is in the marble, the kernel of it. But the thing is the getting it out clean.

It took Lawrence four novels and a long essay to capture *The Rainbow*. I propose to trace this evolutionary process, to consider the part played in it by the *Study of Thomas Hardy*, and to argue for what seems to me a necessary approach to the exploratory nature of Lawrence's imagination.

I

Both *The Rainbow* and *Women in Love* emerged from the same "flippant," even "jeering" [1] little "pot-boiler," [2] begun in order to distract Lawrence from a serious novel which was getting out of hand. In mid-January 1913 at Gargnano, he abandoned the idea of a novel based on the life of Burns, and began *The Insurrection of Miss Houghton,* which eventually became *The Lost Girl.*[3] He thought this "great—so new, so really a stratum deeper than I think anybody has ever gone . . . all analytical—quite unlike *Sons and Lovers,* not

---

"The Marble and the Statue" by Mark Kinkead-Weekes. From Imagined Worlds, Essays in Honor of John Butt, *edited by Ian Gregor and Maynard Mack (London: Methuen & Co. Ltd., 1968), pp. 371–93, 407–10, 412–18. Reprinted by permission of the publisher. The pages reprinted here are only part of the article entitled "The Marble and the Statue: The Exploratory Imagination of D. H. Lawrence."*

[1] *Letters,* ed. Moore, I, pp. 223, 273 (hereafter referred to as "L.M.").

[2] *Letters,* ed. Huxley, p. 115 (hereafter referred to as "L.H."). Also, L.M., I, p. 197. (Letters printed in both editions will be referred to as "L.H., p. . . . ; L.M., p. . . .")

[3] L.H., p. 92; L.M., I, p. 178. Surviving fragments of the Burns novel are printed in Edward Nehls, *D. H. Lawrence: A Composite Biography* (Madison: University of Wisconsin Press, 1957), vol. 1, pp. 184–95.

a bit visualised";[4] and even as he laid it aside after 200 pages, it still lay "next my heart." [5] But it was "*too* improper." [6] So he began instead, about the middle of March, *The Sisters*, "a queer novel which seems to have come by itself." [7] It was flippant because "it was meant to be for the *jeunes filles*," it was jeering because both sisters were Frieda: "*me*, these beastly, superior, arrogant females! Lawrence *hated* me just over the children . . . so he wrote this!" But it did Lawrence "good to theorise myself out, and to depict Frieda's God Almightiness in all its glory," [8] to release his rebellious feelings about her combination of the Prussian aristocrat, the Magna Mater, and Pallas Athene in plaits. "That was the first crude fermenting of the book," he wrote when it was well advanced, "I'll make it into art now." [8] At quite an early stage however the pot-boiler had already become "earnest and painful," [9] because Lawrence was incapable of remaining flippant for long. "I can only write what I feel pretty strongly about, and that, at present, is the relation between men and women." [10] We glimpse what it is like to find one's work changing and deepening under one's hands. "I am doing a novel which I have never grasped. Damn its eyes, there I am at page 145 and I've no notion what it's about . . . it's like a novel in a foreign language I don't know very well." [11] He finished before 11 June[12] and left for a visit to England a few days later, returning to Germany at the beginning of August.

As soon as he could, he began *The Sisters* again, making two false starts, but eventually finding a new basis.[13] Back in Italy, having written 340 pages, he felt that

> The Laocoon writhing and shrieking have gone from my new work, and I think there is a bit of stillness, like the wide, still, unseeing eyes of a Venus of Melos. . . . There is something in the Greek sculpture that any soul is hungry for—something of the eternal stillness that lies under all movement, under all life, like a source, incorruptible and inexhaustible. It is deeper than change, and struggling. So long I have acknowledged only the struggle, the stream, the change. And now I begin

[4] L.H., pp. 111–12; L.M., I, p. 193.
[5] L.H., p. 118; L.M., I, p. 200. Aldington's misreading of this crucial letter in his Introduction to the Heinemann edition of *The Rainbow* has caused much confusion.
[6] L.H., p. 115; L.M., I, p. 197.
[7] L.H., p. 118; L.M., I, p. 200.
[8] L.M., I, pp. 207–8.
[9] L.H., p. 115; L.M., I, p. 197.
[10] L.H., p. 118; L.M., I, p. 200.
[11] L.H., p. 119; L.M., I, p. 203.
[12] L.H., p. 124; L.M., I, p. 209.
[13] L.H., pp. 136–37; L.M., I, p. 223.

to feel something of the source, the great impersonal which never changes
and out of which all change comes.[14]

A new title, *The Wedding Ring*, indicates a new direct concern with
marriage.[15] By 10 January 1914 it was "nearly finished";[16] but at the
end of the month Garnett's criticisms of the first half brought his
own dissatisfaction to a head and he laid the manuscript aside unfinished, to begin all over again. "It was full of beautiful things but
it missed—I knew that it just missed being itself. So here I am, must
sit down and write it out again. I know it is quite a lovely novel really
—you know that the perfect statue is in the marble, the kernel of it.
But the thing is the getting it out clean." [17]

This time there were at least seven false starts before the third
version was properly under way, at much greater length than before.
(These, with the two earlier versions, amounted to "quite a thousand
pages that I shall burn.")[18] By 22 April, however, Lawrence was sure
not only that his relationship with Frieda had "come through," but
that the novel had too, and that there was the closest connection. "I
am sure of this now, this novel. It is a big and a beautiful work. Before, I could not get my soul into it. That was because of the struggle
and the resistance between Frieda and me. Now you will find her and
me in the novel, I think, and the work is of both of us." [19] On 9 May
he recorded her wish to change the title from *The Wedding Ring* to
The Rainbow,[20] and by 16 May it was finished.[21] On 8 June they left
for England where they were married.

Lawrence thought of the work as complete at this stage. Pinker
had negotiated a lucrative contract with a new publisher, Methuen.
Lawrence signed on 1 July[22] and submitted the manuscript, typed
by his friend Dunlop who was British Consul at La Spezia, not only
to Methuen, but also to Kennerley, with a view to publication in the
U.S.A.[23] On 15 July he asked Marsh to lend him Thomas Hardy's
novels and Lascelles Abercrombie's book on Hardy, because he hoped
"to write a little book on Hardy's people." [24]

Early in August came a shattering blow. Methuen returned the

[14] L.M., I, p. 241.
[15] L.H., p. 172; L.M., I, p. 259.
[16] L.H., p. 174.
[17] L.H., p. 179; L.M., I, p. 264.
[18] L.H., pp. 186–87; L.M., I, p. 269.
[19] L.H., p. 189; L.M., I, p. 272.
[20] L.H., p. 193; L.M., I, p. 276.
[21] L.M., I, p. 276.
[22] L.H., p. 200; L.M., I, p. 284.
[23] See Lawrence's letters of 18 September and 18 November, in S. Foster Damon,
Amy Lowell, A Chronicle (Boston, Houghton, 1935), pp. 270, 279.
[24] L.H., p. 205; L.M., I, p. 287.

manuscript as "it could not be published in its then condition." [25]
The future was already casting a long shadow. Lawrence was aghast:
"Here is a state of affairs—what is to become of us?" [26] Quite apart
from his feelings about the novel itself, financial security had changed
in a moment to embarrassment. The war had broken out. It seemed
impossible to go back to Italy. Yet Lawrence seems never to have
considered rewriting to satisfy Methuen. On 5 September he wrote
to Pinker: "What a miserable world. What colossal idiocy, this war.
Out of sheer rage I've begun my book about Thomas Hardy." [27] He
told Amy Lowell on 18 November that it was "supposed to be on
Thomas Hardy, but in reality a sort of Confessions of my heart," and
that he was just finishing.[28]

It is easy to see what attracted Lawrence to the author of *Tess*, and
more especially, *Jude*. He had told Garnett that the germ of his novel
had been, even in the first *Sisters*, "woman becoming individual, self-
responsible, taking her own initiative." [29] But in the same letter he
explained that, although the first *Sisters* had been "flippant, and often
vulgar and jeering," he was primarily "a passionately religious man,
and my novels must be written from the depth of my religious experience." In January 1913, before he began the first *Sisters*, he had written an extraordinary "Preface" to *Sons and Lovers*, never intended
for publication, which is only about *Sons and Lovers* in the same sense
that the *Study of Thomas Hardy* is about Hardy. It is actually a first
attempt to find a formulation for Lawrence's deepest religious con-
victions, by rewriting Christian theology in terms of the relation between man and woman. It announces his belief that the Flesh is made
Word to dwell among us; that Woman lies in travail to give birth to
Man, who in his hour utters his Word. "And God the Father, the
Inscrutable, the Unknowable, we know in the Flesh, in Woman. She
is the door for our in-going and our out-coming. In her we go back
to the Father, but like the witnesses of the Transfiguration, blind and
unconscious." But, as the bee moves between the hive and the flower,
so man must move in a continuous creative rhythm between the source
of his renewal, and his utterance, "the glad cry: 'This is I—I am I.'
And this glad cry when we know, is the Holy Ghost the Comforter." [30]

In the *Study of Thomas Hardy*, Lawrence's religion and his fiction
begin to come together. It is a sustained attempt to work out the

[25] See the report of proceedings at the trial of *The Rainbow*, *Sunday Times*, 14
November 1915, p. 13. (I am indebted for this reference, and much helpful criticism,
to John Worthen.)
[26] L.H., p. 207; L.M., I, p. 289.
[27] L.H., p. 208; L.M., I, p. 290.
[28] Damon, *Amy Lowell*, p. 279.
[29] L.H., p. 190; L.M., I, p. 273.
[30] L.H., pp. 100, 101.

meaning of his earlier intuitions into what could be called, not improperly, a "theology" of marriage—a study of creativity embarked on under the first impact of war. Only then was he able to write *The Rainbow*, the History, or even "Bible," in which that theology is embodied, tested, and further explored imaginatively, in terms of human relationships.

II

Without the manuscripts of the first three novels, we cannot hope to measure fully how far the *Study* took Lawrence beyond *The Wedding Ring*. Fortunately, however, fragments of *Sisters* I and *Sisters* II survive; and Lawrence inserted a section of *The Wedding Ring* into the autograph manuscript of *The Rainbow*.[31] From these we can learn rather more of the growth of the work than the letters tell us.

The first *Sisters* seems to have been an "Ur"-version of *Women in Love*. Lawrence planned a novel of 300 pages. The remaining fragment is numbered 291–6. Gudrun, pregnant with Gerald's child, confronts both Gerald and Loerke in her lodgings in England. Gerald now wants to marry her, but she suspects it may be only because of the baby. Loerke has already offered himself. Even from a bald account, one can see what Lawrence meant by saying the novel was "for the *jeunes filles*," and the style is still a little novelettish, though the flippancy has quite gone. It ends:

> "I shouldn't have cared for any other man's child," she said, slowly.
> He kissed her hands, and they sat still. There was a good deal that
> hurt still, between them. But he was humble to her. Only, she must love
> him—she must love him, or else everything was barren. This aloofness
> of hers—she came to him as the father of her child, not as to a lover, a
> husband. Well he had had a chance, and lost it. He had been a fool.

[31] In the D. H. Lawrence manuscript collection of Texas University; *cf.* Warren Roberts, *A Bibliography of D. H. Lawrence* (London, Hart Davis, 1963), p. 353, entry E441b; p. 346, entry E331a. I identify the first fragment as belonging to *Sisters* I, both on internal evidence of style and pagination, and because it is written on unusually large folio paper of poor quality, presumably Italian, and like that of the manuscript of the "Preface" to *Sons and Lovers*, which is dated Gargnano, January 1913. I identify the second fragment as belonging to *Sisters* II because of the mention of Ben Templeman. The typescript inserted into the autograph manuscript of *The Rainbow*, pp. 219–75 and 279–84, renumbered 548–604 and 608–13, must come from an earlier stage because of the references to Ella and "Charles" Skrebensky, and the writing in of reference to Winifred Inger. *The Wedding Ring* is the only previous version we know to have been typed, by Dunlop, and this typescript is faint enough to be a second carbon. Typescripts of *The Wedding Ring* were submitted both to Methuen and to Kennerley.

Now he must make the best of it, and get her again. But it hurt that she
did not seem to want him very much. It hurt keenly.
    Then while he was thinking, with his forehead hard with pain, she
kissed him, drawing him to her, (?murmuring) "My love!"

Lawrence's theme, in the Gerald/Gudrun story, seems to have been
the conventional Englishman's inability to submit himself to love with
its sacrifice, its tenderness, its suffering. Loerke—"a decent fellow,
really"—accuses Gerald of trusting to his position to play with women,
and to his strength to threaten men. Gerald is forced to see the German's face "broken into lines of real agony, all distorted." He insists
again and again that he "didn't *know*" whether he could love Gudrun.
But in this scene he shows a "queer abstraction," an "unseeing look
in his eyes, as of a creature that follows an instinct blindly, thought-
lessly as a leopard running on in the sunshine, for the sake of running," which his sister Winifred finds "fascinating." Now he can accept humiliation before Loerke, and find tears of tenderness. "He
was something he feared he never could be: he had got something he
had pretended to disbelieve in. And, breathing hard, he knew that
this was his life's fulfilment, and a wave of faith, warm, strong, religious faith, went over him." Only, he is also forced to measure and
accept the damage which his inability to love has caused.
    The story of the other "superior flounder" was, however, almost
certainly the more important, though both were modelled on Frieda.
Presumably, the "jeering" was directed through Ella's lover. (A remark in the letters indicates that this story was written in the first
person.)[32] Ella was certainly positive, not to say opinionated, since
Frieda refers to one of her own tart and sweeping generalizations as
"Ella-ing." But the portrait seems to have become more and more
significant to Lawrence, and it was the problem of understanding how
Ella came to be as she was, through some hurt in her past, that con-
stituted the growing-point.
    Thus the second *Sisters* seems to have been the "Ur"-*Rainbow*.
The fragment is numbered 373–80. Yet it is early in Ella's relationship with Birkin. The second *Sisters* was not then a rewriting of the
first, but rather an attempt to get behind it, into the past. Ella is
leaving Birkin's rooms in the Mill, after an encounter that has left
her "trembling, flushed, ashamed," rebellious, and "as yet free of
him"; while Birkin is "raging." Later, after her parents and the
smaller children have gone on holiday to Scarborough, Ella dreams
and meditates, searching her heart to understand Birkin and her own
feelings. He comes to see her when Gudrun is out at a tennis party.
The "new basis" of the novel can be detected not only in the concern

[32] L.M., I, p. 208.

with how Ella's past has shaped her present, but also in the style. The writing has developed a rhythmic quality, a steady cumulative rhythm quietening the somewhat melodramatic conception of the scene, a new "inner" dimension.

> Then he seemed to be coming to her. Summoning all her self-restraint she put her hand on his arm and said, pleadingly, pathetically:
> "No—no."
> He stood still, silent. She felt his living arm beneath his sleeve. It was torture to her. Suddenly she caught him to her, and hid her face on his breast, crying, in a muffled, tortured voice:
> "Do you love me?"
> She clung to him. But his breast was strange to her. His arms were round her tight, hard, compressing her, he was quivering, rigid, holding her against him. But he was strange to her. He was strange to her, and it was almost agony. He was cold to her, however he held her hard in his power and quivered. She felt he was cold to her. And the quivering man stiffened with desire was strange and horrible to her. She got free again, and, with her hands to her temples, she slid away to the floor at his feet, unable to stand, unable to hold her body erect. She must double up, for she could not bear it. But she got up again to go away. And before she reached the door, she was crouching on the floor again, holding her temples in agony. Her womb, her belly, her heart were all in agony. She crouched together on the floor, crying like some wild animal in pain, with a kind of mooing noise, very dreadful to hear, a sound she was unaware of, that came from her unproduced, out of the depth of her body in torture. For some wild moments the paroxysm continued when she crouched on the ground with her head down, mad, crying with an inarticulate, animal noise. Then suddenly it all stopped. It was gone. Her head was clear. And then she was confused with shame . . . (Birkin) stood white to the gills, with wide dark eyes staring blankly. His heart inside him felt red-hot, so that he panted as he breathed. His mind was blank. He knew she did not feel him any more. He knew he had no part in her, that he was out of place. And he had nothing to say. But gradually he grew a little calmer, his eyes lost their wide, dark, hollow look. He was coming to himself.
> "What did I do?" he asked.

It has of course less to do with Birkin, than with the coming to the surface of the deep bruise inflicted on Ella's inner being, by her earlier love affair. At the same time she is aware "that something was taking place, implicating her with him, which she could never revoke or escape. And blindly, almost shrinking, she lapsed forward." Birkin, too, is afraid. "It seems," he writes, "that everything has come toppling down . . . and here I am entangled in the ruins and fragments of my old life, and struggling to get out. You seem to me some land beyond." At the end of the fragment the two girls, walking by the shore, catch sight of Ella's former lover, Ben Templeman. "A wave of

terror, deep, annihilating, went over her. She knew him without looking: his peculiar, straying walk, the odd separate look about him
which filled her with dread. He still had power over her; he was still
Man to her. She knew he would not see her, because he was rather
short-sighted." It seems clear, however, that the novel was to end
with Ella and Birkin finding their true selves, "the eternal and unchangeable that they are," ceasing to be "strange forms, half-ut-
tered." [33]

The criticisms from Garnett which led to the abandonment of this
novel, seem to have been that the character of Ella was inconsistent;
that the affair with Templeman was "wrong"; and that what Lawrence called the "exhaustive method" meant that the "artistic side"
was "in the background," the scenes not "incorporated" enough.[34]
Lawrence agreed with the first point. He explained that he had made
the mistake of "trying to graft on to the character of Louie the character, more or less, of Frieda." For the young Ella he had used the
rather different personality of the girl to whom he had once been
engaged, and whose father and family were to serve as models for the
Will Brangwens.[35] He also agreed with the second point, while insist-
ing that Ella could not be the girl she had to be "unless she had some
experience of love and of men. . . . Then she must have a love
episode, a significant one. But it must not be a Templeman episode."
He refused however to agree to the criticism of the novel's imaginative mode. He had realized that he could no longer write like *Sons
and Lovers,* "in that hard, violent style full of sensation and presentation." [36] He felt that the new style, even if its "flowers" were "frail
and shadowy," was true to himself in a period of transition. "I pre-
fer the permeating beauty . . . it is not so easy for one to be married.
In marriage one must become something else. And I am changing, one
way or the other." [37] The new style had to feel, like the new man, for
the hidden forces behind the surface drama.

The Wedding Ring brought the second *Sisters* nearer to *The Rainbow,* though it still went well on, into what is now *Women in Love.*
The section that Lawrence thought enough of to incorporate into the
first draft of *The Rainbow,* runs from Ella's first day as a teacher, to
the family's removal to Beldover. It was more simply naturalistic than
it is now, not so thematically heightened, but in essence the same.
Unfortunately, however, since it lies outside the relationships with

[33] L.M., I, p. 242.
[34] See Lawrence's reply, L.H., pp. 177–78; L.M., I, pp. 263–64.
[35] See George H. Ford, *Double Measure* (New York, Holt, Rinehart and Winston,
1965), pp. 116–17.
[36] L.H., p. 172; L.M., I, p. 259.
[37] L.H., p. 178; L.M., I, p. 264.

both lovers—though "Charles" Skrebensky is mentioned—it tells us little about the development of the imaginative mode. Its usefulness is rather that its pagination allows us to guess at the new length and what the novel may have contained. It is numbered 219–84, and represents sections 3–5 of chapter 10 of *The Wedding Ring* and sections 1–4 of chapter 11. We know that the novel was a good deal longer than the second *Sisters* which was planned for roughly 400 pages, autograph.[38] We can deduce from a letter[39] that there were about 150 typescript pages from near the end of the earlier episode with Skrebensky to the final failure. (The 65 pages of typescript must come near the beginning of this section.) There must then have been a link between the break with Skrebensky and the meeting with Birkin. Another letter[40] tells us that there were then a further 80 pages to the point where Lawrence decided to end *The Wedding Ring*. This looks like a novel of 475–500 pages, folio typescript, depending on the length of the linking section between the two love affairs. The significant point would therefore be that two-fifths of the novel would seem to have been devoted to Ella's childhood and girlhood—a high proportion. The most likely explanation is that *The Wedding Ring,* seeking to extend the concern with marriage which had suggested the title to Lawrence near the end of the second *Sisters,* may have begun to build up an account of the marriage of Ella's parents as a contrast both with her failure, and with her success. Since the end-point was presumably the marriage of Ella and Birkin, the rainbow symbol probably pointed chiefly to the dissolution of the bad old world and the promise of the "land beyond." (The idea of the new title arrived when the novel was nearly complete.)[41] *The Wedding Ring* may have included, then, the story of Ella's parents, her childhood and youth, the first girlish affair, Brinsley Street School, the Schofields, University and the second affair with Skrebensky, a return to schoolteaching, and the final finding of themselves of Ella and Birkin. Of the episodes that may have caused the banning of *The Rainbow,* we can say definitely that the last relationship between Anna and Will, and Ursula's relationship with Winifred Inger,[42] were not in the novel; and that

---

[38] By deduction from L.H., p. 144; L.M., I, p. 230, and L.H., p. 172; L.M., I, p. 259. On the greater length of *The Wedding Ring:* L.H., p. 193; L.M., I, p. 275.

[39] L.H., p. 219. This is based on the assumption that Lawrence can roughly predict the final length because he is working from *The Wedding Ring* in the knowledge that *The Rainbow* will end shortly after the final failure with Skrebensky. Page 449 of the autograph manuscript of *The Rainbow* concludes the kissing scene in the church. My calculations of course can only be approximate.

[40] L.H., p. 189; L.M., I, p. 272.

[41] L.H., p. 193; L.M., I, p. 276. 9 May 1914.

[42] The last relationship between Anna and Will is written, in autograph, into the final typescript of *The Rainbow.* Reference to Winifred Inger had to be in-

the handling of the affair with Skrebensky had not struck Lawrence as indiscreet,[43] so that he was dumbfounded at the reaction of his new publisher.

III *Impact of Hardy.*

We may now consider the impact, on this apparently completed novel, of the *Study of Thomas Hardy*. The *Study* was almost finished by 18 November 1914. In late November Lawrence began his novel all over again.[44] By early January he realized that the work would be too vast to remain in one volume.[45] At the beginning of February he was claiming that there would be "no very flagrant love passages." At the end of the month he knew that there would be trouble with Methuen and that the novel would have to be fought for.[46] He finished on 2 March,[47] and when he received the typescript from Viola Meynell,[48] he revised the whole thing extensively once more. What had happened?

Through studying Hardy's art and Hardy's people Lawrence had found a language in which to conceive the impersonal forces he saw operating within and between human beings; involving a new clarification of what the novel he had been trying to write was really *about*; and the discovery of a "structural skeleton" on which to re-found it in a new dimension. The full implications only dawned gradually, but that it was a new dimension is beyond doubt.

Lawrence was impressed by the way that Hardy's figures moved against a vast impersonal landscape.

There is a constant revelation in Hardy's novels: that there exists a great background, vital and vivid, which matters more than the people who move upon it. . . . This is the wonder of Hardy's novels, and gives

---

serted into the typescript from *The Wedding Ring* incorporated into the autograph manuscript.

[43] As late as 1 February 1915, six months after the rejection of *The Wedding Ring*, and when he had written 450 pages of *The Rainbow*, Lawrence assures Pinker that there will be "no very flagrant love passages in it (at least to my way of thinking)," L.H., p. 219. This *might* suggest that the beach scene had not yet occurred to him either.

[44] He had written "the first hundred or so pages" by 5 December 1914, L.H., p. 212; L.M., I, p. 296.

[45] L.M., I, p. 306.

[46] L.M., I, pp. 316, 322.

[47] L.M., I, pp. 327, 328.

[48] The typing was done by two people, Viola Meynell farming out part of it to a Miss K. Lee in Harrow. (See the note on the back of p. 495 of the autograph manuscript.)

them their beauty. The vast unexplored morality of life itself, what we call the immorality of nature, surrounds us in its eternal incomprehensibility, and in its midst goes on the little human morality play.[49]

Its true "moral" is that man "at least must learn to be at one, in his mind and will, with the primal impulses that rise in him." [50]

Hardy must consequently have reinforced his understanding of his own new style. Before he began the *Study* he had already made a well known defence of the "psychology" of *The Wedding Ring* in answer to Garnett.

You mustn't look in my novel for the old stable *ego* of the character. There is another *ego,* according to whose action the individual is unrecognisable, and passes through, as it were, allotropic states which it needs a deeper sense than any we've been used to exercise, to discover are states of the same single radically unchanged element . . . the characters fall into the form of some other rhythmic form, as when one draws a fiddle-bow across a fine tray delicately sanded, the sand takes lines unknown.[51]

The "characters" in Hardy exist in terms of being and consciousness, rather than the conduct of "the old stable ego." [52] In *Sons and Lovers* Lawrence's people had already opened into dimensions of being, but had retained a recognisable density springing partly from autobiography, and partly from the mode, "that hard, violent style full of sensation and presentation." The development of *The Wedding Ring* out of the first *Sisters* had taken Lawrence steadily further away from autobiographical material, and *The Rainbow* was to take him further still. His reading of Hardy must have taught him a great deal about the presentation of beings, related to the great background of nature, embodied in concretely rendered physical existence and consciousness, yet capable of revealing the "allotropic" play of the impersonal forces that were to be the deepest concern of *The Rainbow*. The first of its three stories, and the deepest dimension of the other two, could not have been achieved before the *Study*.

As he pondered "Hardy's people," moreover—Eustacia, Tess, Angel, Alec, and especially Arabella, Jude, and Sue—his whole understanding of the impersonal forces that operated within and between men and women began to be clarified, extended, deepened. He took up the intuitions of the "Preface" to *Sons and Lovers* and made a sustained effort to explore them imaginatively. The *Study* is not a philosophical

[49] Edward D. McDonald, ed., *Phoenix—The Posthumous Papers of D. H. Lawrence* (London, Heinemann, 1936), p. 419.

[50] *Phoenix*, p. 418.

[51] L.H., pp. 198–99; L.M., I, p. 282.

[52] See Ian Gregor, "What Kind of Fiction Did Hardy Write?" *Essays in Criticism* (July 1966), pp. 290–308.

work, nor a work of literary criticism, since Hardy is only what started it off. It is primarily a work of "religious" imagination, and secondarily an essential stage in the discovery of what he had been trying to write about since *Sons and Lovers*—the creativity of marriage.

Lawrence tries to formulate in the *Study* a way of looking at every personality and all relationships as the outcome of conflict between two radically opposed forces, impersonal, and universal.[53] Both are vital to creative growth; and though they are separable for the sake of understanding, they are ultimately one, as the movement at the rim of a wheel and the stillness at its centre are one. He continually refers to these forces as "Male" and "Female," but we must not simply translate into "Man" and "Woman." The *Study* sometimes invites confusion, being exploratory, but it is clear enough that "Male" and "Female" both exist and conflict within every man and woman, as well as between them. We need also to be clear that sex is essentially a religious mystery to Lawrence, the one way he knows and believes in, by which human beings can contact "the beyond": "the sexual act . . . is for leaping off into the unknown, as from a cliff's edge." [54] Sexuality as such is not essential. "What we call the Truth is, in actual experience, that momentary state when in living the union between the male and the female is consummated. This consummation may be also physical, between the male body and the female body. But it may be only spiritual, between the male and female spirit." [55] In order to avoid confusion, and register the religious dimension of Lawrence's imagination, we would be well advised to use his own alternative terminology. The "Female" is the force of *Law*, of *God the Father*. The "Male" is the force of *Love*, of *God the Son.*

Through the lives of all men and women there operates a creative conflict between these two great impersonal forces. God the Father is immutable, all-embracing, one. By his Law, life is pure being, in complete unity with the universe of created things. Man exists in the flesh, in nature, in sensation. All creation is one whole. To exist is to be in togetherness. But equally there operates throughout creation the force of God the Son, which is Love. Love however does not mean what we expect it to mean. It is the impulse to move from being to knowing, from undifferentiated oneness to perception of what is not-self, and to define the self by this process into individuality. So Love is the force of differentiation into the many, into separateness, into consciousness, and ultimately into self-expression and art. The ideal of Love is to move into ever more complete individuation.

[53] H. M. Daleski, *The Forked Flame* (London, Faber, 1965) is the first account of the importance of the *Study* for the interpretation of the novels.
[54] *Phoenix*, p. 441.
[55] Ibid., p. 460.

These two forces are necessarily locked in eternal conflict. There can be no final victory, and no assertion that one is better than the other, for the conflict is necessary to growth. It is, in other words, not dualistic but implicitly dialectic, since it always implies a state beyond every successive clash of thesis and antithesis. Beyond God the Father and God the Son, and the battle between Law and Love, is God the Holy Spirit, the Comforter. There is not only collision but consummation, marriage. Now

> that which is mixed in me becomes pure, that which is female in me is given to the female, that which is male in her draws to me, I am complete, I am pure male, she is pure female, we rejoice in contact naked and perfect and clear, singled out into ourselves, and given the surpassing freedom. No longer do we see through a glass darkly. For she is she and I am I, and clasped together with her I know how perfectly she is not me, how perfectly I am not her, how utterly we are two, the light and the darkness, and how infinitely and eternally not-to-be-comprehended by either of us is the surpassing One we make. Yet of the One, this incomprehensible, we have an inkling that satisfies us.

That this is a theology, the next sentence will suffice to show: "Through Christ Jesus I know that I shall find my Bride when I have overcome the impurity of the Flesh. When the Flesh in me is put away, I shall embrace the Bride, and I shall know as I am known." [56]

There can however be no stasis, only a never-ending process. Lawrence sees all the inner history of mankind in religion and art as a set of variations on the same eternal dialectic. Within marriage, the whole point is that the lovers should open up for each other an infinite unknown, an infinite beyond. Lawrence vilified the "one-flesh" idea of marriage precisely because it suggested completion, the merging of opposites. Conflict remains vital; if one force ever wins or the other collapses the consummation is crippled. There must be neither submission nor over-assertion, neither too-female being nor too-male knowing. Battle is the condition of growth but the aim is to "come through," ever *beyond*.

What we watch is Lawrence in the act of trying to formulate a "theoretical" basis for his whole intuitive view of marriage, and in the process beginning to clarify what it was that his fiction had been trying to express. But we can also see him reaching in the *Study* for a new form, as well as a more articulate grasp of his subject. As his "theology" reinterpreted Judaism and Christianity, so he found in the sacred history in which their theology had been embodied, a hint of the shape his own "bible" ought to have, and a hint of the point at which it should end. "Always the threefold utterance: the declar-

[56] Ibid., p. 468.

ing of the God seen approaching, the rapture of contact, the anguished joy of remembrance, when the meeting has passed into separation." [57] Refining on this, he cites the story of David as an example of the first phase, Solomon for the second, Job for the third. Then in discussing Solomon he shows that the rapture of contact turns into rupture, because the man is too weak and the woman conquers; but since there had been real contact, "the living thing was conserved, kept always alive and powerful, but restrained, restricted, partial."

This is why the new novel had to have three stories or "testaments": a beautiful but partial old world, in Old Testament style; a world of transition in which fulfilment is fused with failure, and the promised land is seen but not entered; a new world of maximum separation almost unto death, but retaining in extremity the memory of an abiding covenant. The *Study* would eventually show Lawrence where to end *The Rainbow* by removing all the Birkin material, changing a conclusion of affirmation to near-tragedy, but retaining an anguished joy in separation. It showed him where to begin, with a new story of a world dominated by God the Father, that his understanding of Hardy's art must have helped him to handle. *The Rainbow* was almost certainly written backwards; the story of Tom and Lydia being the last to take shape, with the others being filled out thematically against its perspective. That is why, after cutting all the *Women in Love* material, the novel is so much longer than *The Wedding Ring*. The *Study* also shows us why there is such continual reference to the Bible—(particularly the Noah story, the journeying Israelites, and the search for a son of God by a daughter of Man); why there is also such a wealth of theological language; and why *The Rainbow* reinterprets Biblical history and theology in so very different a light.

Before we leave the *Study*, however, we should also note the significance of Lawrence's application of his theory to Art. It too must contain a dialectic of opposites, a real conflict in which both sides are allowed to assert themselves fully, and the scales are never weighted. Furthermore it must both Be and Know—must contain, as it were, a continual "systole and diastole" of poetry and analytic prose, exploration and understanding. Most of all, the Supreme Art must move through thesis and antithesis to try to see beyond. There is an Art "which recognises and utters (a man's) own law," that is, his own being; and an Art "which recognises his own and also the law of the woman, his neighbour, utters the glad embraces and the struggle between them, and the submission of one," that is, where a man pits his own vision against an antithesis, which it overcomes. "But the

[57] Ibid., p. 450.

supreme art is one which knows the two conflicting laws, and knows
the final reconciliation, where both are equal, two in one, complete."
This, he says, "remains to be done. Some men have attempted it and
left the remains of efforts. But it remains to be done." [58] *The Rainbow*
is an attempt at a supreme fiction, aiming at a wisdom which will not
criticize one side of any conflict and not the other. Lawrence is critical
of both Anna and Will, cogently critical of Ursula when we read him
sensitively, not only of Skrebensky. Similarly, the imaginative exploration of Birkin in *Women in Love* aims at mature self-criticism, not
mere self-assertion, and the treatment of Gerald and Gudrun is fully
complex, cutting, and tender.

This in turn helps to make an essential point about the relation
of the *Study* to the novel it enabled Lawrence to write. The *Study*
allowed him to see that "every novel must have the background or the
structural skeleton of some theory of being, some metaphysic";[59] for
that is exactly what he had provided for himself. On the other hand,
having also understood how essential it is that the highest form of
art should be a true unweighted conflict, an exploration not an assertion, his next sentence goes on to insist that "the metaphysic must
always subserve the artistic purpose *beyond the artist's conscious aim*
(my italics). Otherwise the novel becomes a treatise." The *Study* is
the "structural skeleton" of *The Rainbow*; but it is not a skeleton
key and must not be misused as one. It is the greatest of commentaries
on what the novel is fundamentally *about,* but it is a treatise, and
The Rainbow is not. When its "ideas" come to be embodied in human
relationships, the basic insight is tested out, explored, and extended,
with an enormous increase in subtlety and complexity. Lawrence was
a novelist, not a philosopher, and the *Study* turned out to be only a
stage, if a very important one, in the growth of a novel. *The Rainbow* discovers new themes, like that of death and resurrection: the
way that the marriage of opposites involves a "death" of the pre-
existing selves and a rebirth into a new state, the Resurrection, or
Paradise, or the Heavens. (Though the "pale Galilean" had played an
essential role in the *Study,* curiously His death and resurrection had
not.) The novel is thus more explicitly dialectic than the treatise had
been. Most obvious of all: when the imagination of Lawrence the
novelist is liberated in its proper medium, he creates people and situations whose density extends far beyond the categories of his "thinking."

[58] Ibid., pp. 515–16.
[59] Ibid., p. 479. See also the interesting aside about Hardy and his "metaphysic,"
L.H., p. 120; L.M., I, p. 204, as early as the first *Sisters.*

IV

The evolution of one of *The Rainbow*'s greatest scenes, the episode in Lincoln Cathedral, will show how the imaginative exploration grows out of the *Study*. At a very late stage in composition, moreover, the novel remains fluid in Lawrence's imagination, which finds it necessary to move on, by its own kind of "logic," to a stage quite beyond the scope of the treatise.

The Cathedral scene was not in *The Wedding Ring*, since we can watch Lawrence in the first draft of *The Rainbow* struggling to get hold of it, and failing at first.[60] He had grasped the contrast between the marriage of Tom and Lydia and the young married life of Anna and Will, and had summed it up in terms of his dominant image: in one case, the pillar of fire and the pillar of cloud locked into an arch, creating freedom, and a gateway to the beyond; in the other, the rich woman possessing her husband, settled on Pisgah, still within sight of the rainbow and the promised land, but capable only of being a threshold from which her children can set forth, because she has conquered.

Lawrence must have felt, however, that he needed to explore the religious dimension of the marriage further, beyond merely personal relationship—even when "personal" is defined at the depth of a chapter like "Anna Victrix." In the *Study*, as part of a long account of the spiritual dialectic in art, he had briefly remarked on the mediaeval cathedrals:

> The worship of Europe, predominantly female, all through the mediaeval period, was to the male, to the incorporeal Christ, as a bridegroom, whilst the art produced was the collective, stupendous emotional gesture of the Cathedrals, where a blind collective impulse rose into concrete form. It was the profound, sensuous desire and gratitude which produced an art of architecture, whose essence is in utter stability, of movement resolved and centralized, of absolute movement, that has no relationship with any other form, that admits the existence of no other form, but is conclusive, propounding in its sum the One Being of All.
>
> There was, however, in the Cathedrals, already the denial of the Monism which the Whole uttered. All the little figures, the gargoyles, the imps, the human faces, whilst subordinated within the Great Conclusion of the Whole, still, from their obscurity, jeered their mockery of the Absolute, and declared for multiplicity, polygeny.[61]

[60] Autograph manuscript, pp. 298–310, Texas University Collection (Roberts, *Bibliography*, p. 346, entry E331a).

[61] *Phoenix*, p. 454.

Lawrence's first attempt to realize this within the response of his human characters was, as one might expect, rather gushing and repetitive, allowing his imagination free rein. Will's response is a good deal longer than it is now, aiming again and again at the same target. The church is a great darkness and silence, a "dark rainbow," a "link of darkness" between the eternity before birth and the eternity after death. It is "away from time, always away from life." The repetition is not however merely repetitive; for Lawrence tries to create a succession of passionate leapings up from the "plain earth" to the "stud of ecstasy" at the roof, that point of tension where the "immemorial darkness" is both thrust up, and weighs back—again, and again, and again as the eye passes down the nave towards the "other mystery" of the altar.

In the same manuscript, he revised extensively with a new conception. Now the church is not outside life, it is the womb within which all life is implicit. Light begins to enter, a twilight, yet "the embryo of all light." The church lies

> like a seed in silence, dark before germination, silenced after death. Containing birth and death, potential with all the noise and transition of life, the cathedral remained hushed, a great involved seed whereof the flower would be radiant life inconceivable, but whose beginning and whose end lay in the two extremes of silence. Like a shadowy rainbow, the jewelled gloom spanned from silence to silence, darkness to darkness, fecundity to fecundity, as a seed spans from life to life and death to death, containing the secret of all folded between its parts.[62]

He cut about a page and a half, began to discipline, condense, heighten.

The more significant growth however is in the response of Anna. We can tell little about the first version, since all but a few sentences were deleted[63] and replaced when Lawrence revised Will's response, but "she too was overcome," though she resisted. In revision, she is at first carried away almost as much as Will; only she is not fulfilled. For her soul longs to "be cast at last on the threshold of the unknown," at the altar, but always she is made to leap "to the ecstasy and the isolation and the agony up there." That night, she becomes increasingly dissatisfied, seeing the experience as a kind of crucifixion of self-knowledge. And again she longs for the march of the great pillars down the nave to the threshold of the unknown. She dreams of angels, flaming in praise around the presence of God. But when they go back to the cathedral the next day, there is no getting beyond self-realization, no transfiguration of the stigmata of self-knowledge, no door to

---

[62] Autograph manuscript, p. 300.
[63] See the foot of autograph manuscript p. 302.

the beyond. She is shut in. Even if she thinks of the smallness of man's ego against the "whole rotunda of day or the dome of night" there is no help, for "which star should she choose?" In the cathedral the altar is "a dragged nest, the Mystery was gone." She longs to take off like a bird, "to rise into the gladness of light . . . to escape from the builded earth, from man's day after day. Was man and his present measure to be forever the measure of the universe? But she must grasp at some resistance before she could thrust off. It was so difficult." So she grasps at the little faces.

At his second attempt, then, Lawrence has used the images thrown off in a remark in the *Study*—"the column must always stand for the male aspiration, the arch or ellipse for the female completeness containing this aspiration" [64]—but has made the "male" aspiration of Anna aspire beyond the "completeness" which satisfies Will. The march of the columns is succeeded by the flight of the bird from the dragged nest, towards the sun. The trouble is that the opposition is simple, and furthermore, by making Anna go through Will's experience before rejecting it, Lawrence has weighted the scales in her favour. She seems to know more than he does. There had been at the end of the previous chapter a similar tendency to lay too much stress on the failure of Will. As Lawrence had corrected that, so he now labours to correct this, and to complicate and intensify the oppositions while leaving the balance unweighted.

So in the final manuscript of *The Rainbow* he begins to introduce opposites within Will's response, as well as tightening the style into greater cogency. The sentence I quoted from the first draft now becomes:

> Spanned around with the rainbow, the jewelled gloom folded music upon silence, light upon darkness, fecundity upon death, as a seed folds leaf upon leaf and silence upon the root and the flower, hushing up the secret of all between its parts, the death out of which it fell, the life into which it has dropped, the immortality it involves, and the death it will embrace again.[65]

He also removes altogether the march down the aisle, so that Will's response is now wholly concerned with the ecstasy of the arch, the "female" completeness and inclusiveness of God the Father, in which, as in the natural seed, all is One.

But he transforms Anna's response. She is now resentful from the very first, in greater opposition; and she opposes to him not the "blue vault" of the sky nor the "dark dome" of night, "but a space where

---

[64] *Phoenix*, p. 460.
[65] Penguin edition, pp. 201–2. (This reprint of the "banned" first edition is much the best text available.)

stars were whirling in freedom, with freedom above them ever
higher." She resists the march to the altar, and catches at the little
faces not as something to thrust off from, but as something "which
saved her from being swept headlong." She resolves the opposition
within her in a far more antireligious fashion. The faces which had
been merely human "with their nice and nasty traits" become
"wicked," the serpent of Knowledge in the Eden of God the Father.
And she becomes like them, jeering, malicious, but more so: she
triumphs not only in multiplicity, but in destruction.

It has become a far more complex conflict, and deeper. We no
longer take sides. Both lovers have half the truth, but their conflict
is destructive, for they do not marry their oppositions and go through,
beyond. Will's arches, his rainbow, contain conflict resolved, but on
too limited a level. Anna aspires to a higher freedom and space,
greater multiplicity and separateness, but she seeks to destroy her
opposite. The new dimension Lawrence has achieved also allows us
to balance the contrast with Tom and Lydia more fairly. We can
measure how much more "paradisal" the earlier marriage had been;
how Tom and Lydia rejoiced in the "otherness" of each other; but
how they were also prepared to "die" to each other in marriage, and
be reborn into a new world beyond. On the other hand, we can now
see more clearly that the new intensities of Anna and Will, while
making the marriage of opposites more difficult to achieve, also show
up the limitations of Tom and Lydia. Will's religious and aesthetic
intensity, Anna's rational intelligence and self-awareness, represent a
greater range of human possibility as well as difficulty. So the growth
of the Cathedral scene shows us Lawrence's exploratory imagination
feeling for one of his great achievements, beginning from the insights
and categories of the *Study*, but creating a richness and complexity
beyond the scope of the treatise.

In the novel as we have it, however, the relationship between Anna
and Will passes through yet another stage, in which we can see Lawrence reaching for a new kind of insight altogether. These episodes
were not only not in *The Wedding Ring*, they were not in the first
draft of *The Rainbow* either. There, Lawrence spoke only briefly of
"some months" in which Anna

> let herself go, she gave him also his full measure, she considered noth-
> ing. Children and everything she let go, and gave way to her last desires,
> till she and he had gone all the devious and never-to-be-recorded ways
> of desire and satisfaction, to the very end, till they had had everything,
> and knew no more. Whatever their secret imagination had wanted,
> they had. And they came through it all at last cleared, resolved, freed.

They were not ashamed of any of it. They were now resolved into satisfaction. They had taken every liberty, were prisoners to no more lurking desires. The marriage between them was complete and entire.[66]

In the final draft of *The Rainbow,* a page or two expand into half a chapter. Will's escapade with the factory girl in Nottingham is new, and there is an odd new dimension in the treatment of the change between Will and Anna.

From the stage of the second *Sisters* at least, Lawrence had been becoming more and more aware of the importance of *impersonality* for his conception of marriage. In the *Study* he had discovered a language for talking about the impersonal forces that operated within and between human beings. In the Tom and Lydia story, successful marriage had depended to a great extent on the utter strangeness and foreignness of the lovers to each other, and their delight in the battle of "others," opening the door to the unknown. In the Anna and Will story, Will is at first utterly strange too, like another form of life, a cat, a hawk; but by the end of "Anna Victrix" he is known, possessed. He can no longer open out the unknown.

Now, through the adventure of writing the "dark" relationship between Ursula and Skrebensky when he returns from Africa, Lawrence had achieved a new insight into what he would call the "African Way" of relationship in *Women in Love.* He must have seen, in that last sketched-in relationship of Anna and Will, an opportunity both to complete the range of their story, and to emphasize with a new insistence, and in a new way, the essential significance of "otherness" and "impersonality." It is the peculiarity of the insistence that has made this last relationship seem odd to critics; but if imagination may be spoken of as having a "logic," it is a logical extension of a growing insight.

The point of the episode with the warehouse girl is that the two are utterly alien, with nothing in common except sexuality, and that Will cares nothing about the girl as a person. Just because of this, a new word begins to be used. "He was himself, the *absolute,* the rest of the world was an object that should contribute to his being." "And his hand that grasped her side felt one curve of her, and it seemed like a new creation to him, a reality, an absolute, an existing tangible beauty of the absolute." The girl will not give herself to him, but in the roused state she has excited he suddenly becomes again to Anna "a strange man come home to her." At last, and on a new level, "she replied with a brilliant challenge . . . she challenged him back with a sort of radiance, very bright and free, opposite to him. . . . It was as if he were a perfect stranger, as if she were in-

---

[66] Autograph manuscript, p. 341.

finitely and essentially strange to him." They become discoverers, and
what they discover is "Absolute Beauty."

This new relationship is, however, sharply distinguished from their
relation as lovers. It exists entirely in terms of lust. It begins in pure
sexual challenge, abandoning morality, responsibility, above all, personality. It issues in "a sensuality violent and extreme as death. They
had no conscious intimacy, no tenderness of love. It was all the lust
and the infinite, maddening intoxication of the senses, a passion of
death." Their lust not only now explicitly embraces the shameful and
unnatural, but also finds in this a "sinister tropical beauty," a "heavy,
fundamental gratification." (Wilson Knight is clearly correct in claiming that imagery and language identify the "unnatural" element as
anal.[67] It is a relation in "pure darkness," quite different from the
marriage of opposites that is central to the book.

Lawrence clearly does not endorse this in the way he endorses the
marriage of Tom and Lydia. Yet, equally significantly, he cannot be
said to condemn it either. Whatever the private reactions of readers
may be, it is important to notice how this relationship achieves things
for Will and Anna that their loving relationship, in its partial failure,
had withheld. They discover absolute beauty; become explorers. They
find themselves without destroying each other; and for the first time
they set each other free. Anna is recalled from her trance of motherhood to live more in herself, not through her children, and to take
an interest in the outside world; and Will is not only more founded
in himself but actually liberated into public activity. He not only
takes up his art again but becomes a teacher, with a role in society.
The first draft of the novel briefly sketched in these results, but we
have now been provided with a somewhat startling reason for them.

The beauty is absolute as opposed to relative, because it is impersonal, pursued for its own sake. It has nothing to do with the personality. Anna and Will not only find it, but create it together, as a
third thing beyond themselves. Will ceases to be a known, finite being to Anna. She meets him on equal terms at last; does not try to
overcome or destroy him; is as ready to abandon herself to him as he
to her. There is no defeat or victory, dominance or subservience.
There is discovery, and there is freedom. We see how absolutely central to Lawrence his concern for the freedom of the individual turns
out to be, and how far he is prepared to go to insist on it. Because
they meet at last as distinct individuals, enriching themselves from
each other rather than merging or battling for supremacy, even this
relation in pure darkness can have beneficial results never achieved
by the two as lovers.

[67] Wilson Knight, "Lawrence, Joyce, and Powys," *Essays in Criticism* (October
1961), pp. 403–17.

Which is not to say, of course, that we are meant to see it as an equal alternative.[68] In pure darkness there can be no marriage of total opposites, and hence there can be no transformation. Anna and Will are only more firmly settled into their existing selves; they are not transfigured, inheriting a promised land of re-creation. They "die" and are renewed, but it is "pure death" purely dark, and a renewal of the dark side of themselves only. A great part of their total personalities has to be excluded. Using the "carbon" metaphor with which Lawrence defended his new psychology against Garnett, we might say that the relation of lust is, to the relation of love, as jet is to the diamond that is produced by the interaction of black carbon with intense flame. Nevertheless, in this limited relationship, Will and Anna can confront each other in *some* of the ways essential to Lawrence's conception of a fruitful relationship, as they seemed incapable of doing as lovers. Because of this, the relation in lust can enrich and set free. Perhaps there is more concern with sexuality itself than elsewhere; but this, too, is a precise pointer to the limitation of the Dark Way. Even here it is a Way, a means to an end. It is still the end, of individual growth and individual freedom, that is the main concern.

V

We have some idea now of what the word "exploratory" means, against the perspective of the whole process of creation from the first *Sisters*. We have also seen that his theory of art was essentially a theory of process. But I want now to argue that "process" is absolutely central to Lawrence's imagination itself: that we shall not respond fully to his best work until we learn to read in terms of process. There is a tendency to give too static an account of Lawrence's "symbols." Even in highly sophisticated accounts of scenes like the episode with the horses in *The Rainbow* one can detect that the basic question has been "What do the horses stand for?" or, more subtly, "What *are* they?" I want to argue that criticism on such a basis can only establish part, and that not the essential part, of the imaginative vision that is operating.

Ursula's story in *The Rainbow* has shown her embodying all the "opposites" of her family at peak intensity, but forever trying to re-

[68] Colin Clarke reprimands me for "moralising" here (*River of Dissolution*, p. 52). Yet it seems very clear to me that the structure of *The Rainbow* is comparative, and that if we compare this relationship (or Ursula's "dark" one with Skrebensky) with the marriage of opposites in Tom and Lydia, or with the potentialities open to Will and Anna in the corn-stacking scene, the verdict is as I state it.

solve her contradictions by pursuing one element of herself to the exclusion of others, never managing to find a way of marrying them—"always the shining doorway was a gate into another ugly yard, dirty and active and dead." She has ended by destroying Skrebensky, destroying even his potential for the Dark Way in which alone he could find fulfilment. Her remorse over her own selfish destructiveness is justified; but in seeking, in reaction, to reduce herself to her mother's domesticity, she denies the deepest most aspiring impulse of her own being. She has tried all the wrong ways. Only the right way remains, and Lawrence proceeds to confront her with its challenge in the inevitable climax of the book, that mysterious, difficult, but intensely powerful and haunting scene with the horses.

To ask "what" confronts Ursula is certainly to tap a part of the scene's rich significance, though even here no adequate answer will emerge from trying to expound the horses alone. The scene confronts the girl who is ready to deny the elemental forces in herself and settle for the ordinary civilized world of domesticity, with the powerful presence of those forces and their eternal challenge. The sophisticated, intelligent, educated, self-conscious daughter of Man, of the Prospect, and the City, is faced with the forces of the unitary Landscape of Nature, of God the Father: the big wind through which her grandfather walked, the earth and its roaring trees, the teeming rain, the looming power of the animal world that Tom so confidently mastered, the fire from their nostrils. But the summons is not to the simply elemental; it is to the complexity of the marriage of opposites. The birdsoul of the aspiring girl comes to the great Hall of the Warriors, attesting the eternity of battle; but she searches also for a lost stability beyond conflict and flux. If we then look through Ursula's eyes, we begin to see what Lawrence has embodied in the horses: She becomes

> aware of their breasts gripped, clenched narrow in a hold that never relaxed, she was aware of their red nostrils flaming with long endurance, and of their haunches, so rounded, so massive, pressing, pressing, pressing to burst the grip upon their breasts, pressing forever till they went mad, running against the walls of time and never bursting free. Their great haunches were smoothed and darkened with rain. But the darkness and wetness of rain could not put out the hard, urgent, massive fire that was locked within these flanks, never, never.

What the elemental world embodies and reveals is the eternal clash of opposites in all created things. The horses are an intensity of conflict that cannot be denied or reduced—and must not be, in Ursula. Always the rain tries to put the fire out; always the fire must remain unquenched, battling against the rain. It is the opposition that makes the horses what they are, gives them their looming, monumental energy. But the horses are also gripped, clenched, unfinished. Their opposing energies are trying to get free. And if the fire could once pass right through the rain, and the rain right through the fire, there would be . . . a rainbow. So the horses re-state imaginatively to Ursula, and to us, the whole challenge to marry the Opposites that were embodied in the novel's opening pages.

Yet this is only part, and not the essential part, of the scene's power and meaning. For if we allow Lawrence's imagination to lead us, we shall see that the main question is not "what confronts Ursula?" but "what *happens* to Ursula?" To answer it, we have to respond to what is essentially a process. What happens, happens stage by stage, and if we respond to its "rhythmic" development, what we watch is Ursula confronting the challenge, and failing to meet it. In its simplest terms the challenge is, as ever, to meet the Other and pass through into the Beyond, but this must also mean a marriage of opposites in oneself that involves a kind of death and a kind of rebirth. Now, in the first "movement" of the scene, Ursula does succeed in going through, bursting the barrier of the Other. We have, however, to note the condition for this success. She walks with bent head, not looking, not thinking, not knowing. She simply follows her feet blindly and instinctively. Only in that way does she succeed in coming through the crucible, where her nerves and veins "ran hot, ran white hot, they must fuse, and she must die." This is the condition of Tom and Lydia, the old dispensation, unconscious, unaware. But, in the act of bursting through, the modern woman is forced to *know,* and the repetition of the words "know" and "aware," over and over again, marks the crucial point. We have seen continually in Ursula's story how it is her conscious awareness of her intensities that has made her predicament the hardest of all in the novel. So it proves here. As she passes the horses, and they pass her again, she is forced to know them. As they work themselves up for a climactic confrontation, she will be forced, this time, to go through in full awareness. And she cannot do it. She is terrified, her limbs turn to water, she climbs the tree, and collapses. Instead of going through, she lapses into the element of water alone, becomes unconscious, inert, unchanging, unchangeable, like a stone at the bottom of the stream. This is her "Flood." She fails, and failing almost dies literally, as well as inwardly.

On the physical and psychological level this is adequately explained. She has suffered a terrible shock, and exposure, and miscarries. This is also "symbolically" appropriate, that the child of Ursula and Skrebensky should be an abortive birth. But on a deeper level Lawrence is asserting that Ursula has failed, not only because of the inadequacies of Skrebensky, but because she herself is incapable of the marriage of opposites. She has to "die" to her assertive will, to burst all the "rind" of unrealities and false relations within which her egotism

has enclosed her, to trust herself as a naked kernel does to the elemental forces, before a "true" self can be born. The world she is then
born into is the mysterious work of divine creation, and she lands
on its boundary after crossing chaos: an "undiscovered land" where
she recognizes only "a fresh glow of light and inscrutable trees going
up from the earth like smoke." She is only on the outmost perimeter,
but she is there, on the first Day of her Creation. She must no longer
try to manipulate herself or others or relationships; she must wait
for the coming of a son of God, from the infinite and eternal to
which she now belongs, "within the scope of that vaster power, in
which she rested at last." The covenant of the rainbow can only be
seen by the reborn soul that has "died" to its old self in the Flood.

If one regards such a novel as a "supreme fiction," it is not simply
because of the huge imaginative effort that went into its shaping, or
the power of embodying, testing, and exploring "ideas" in fiction.
It is chiefly because Lawrence aspired to, and achieved in his finest
moments, an imaginative vision inclusive enough to allow all opposites play. The aim of the exploratory theory, and the finest achievement of the exploratory process, are the same: the battle through
partiality and assertion to become objective enough, to make the
"statues" stand free.

Chronology of Important Dates

Life of Lawrence	Literary Career
1885 David Herbert Lawrence born in Eastwood, Nottinghamshire, youngest son of a coal miner.	
1898–1901 Scholarship student at Nottingham High School. Meets Jessie Chambers ("Miriam").	
1901–2 Clerk in Nottingham factory (1901); serious attack of pneumonia (winter).	
1902–6 Pupil-teacher at Eastwood and Ilkeston; unofficial engagement to Jessie Chambers (1904).	First poems (1905); first play (1906).
1906–8 Reads for teacher's certificate at Nottingham University.	Begins *The White Peacock* (1906); first stories (1907).
1908–11 Teaches at Davidson Road School, Croydon; breaks "betrothal" to Jessie Chambers (1910); mother dies (December 1910); seriously ill (winter 1911).	Stories accepted by *The English Review* (1909); writes *The Trespasser* (1910); begins "Paul Morel" (October 1910); *The White Peacock* published (1910).
1912–19 Elopes to Germany with Mrs. Frieda Von Richthofen Weekley (May 1912); in Italy with Frieda (August 1912–June 1914); visits Germany and England (1913); meets Middleton Murray and Katherine Mansfield; marries Frieda in England (July 13, 1914); ill again (Autumn 1914); meets Lady Ottoline Morell and Bertrand Russell (1915); moves to Cornwall	*Sons and Lovers* (begun as "Paul Morel," rewritten, 1912) published (1913); *The Rainbow* (begun as "The Sisters," 1913) published (1915); police seize copies of *The Rainbow* (November 1915); publisher withdraws novel; *Women in Love* (begun as "The Sisters," 1913) rewritten (1916); writes *Aaron's Rod* (1917–19).

(1915); expelled from Cornwall (1917); lives in Berkshire and Derbyshire (1917–19); leaves for Italy (late 1919).

1920–25   Lives in Sicily (March 1920–February 1922); sails to Ceylon and Australia; arrives in Taos, New Mexico (September 1922); lives in New Mexico (to 1925); trips to Mexico, visit to England (1923); near-fatal illness (February 1925); learns he has tuberculosis; revisits Italy and Germany; settles in Italy (to 1928).

Women in Love published (1920); *The Lost Girl* (begun as "The Insurrection of Miss Houghton," 1913) published (1920); *Aaron's Rod* (rewritten 1920–21) published (1922); *Kangaroo* (written 1922) published (1923); writes *The Plumed Serpent* (1923–25).

1926–29   Visits England for last time (1926); authorities seize two manuscripts in mail (January 1929); police confiscate pictures from Warren Gallery (July 1929); lives in Switzerland, France, Majorca, Italy, Germany (1928–29).

The Plumed Serpent published (1926); *Lady Chatterley's Lover* (written 1926–28) published privately by Lawrence in Florence (1928).

1930   Admitted to sanatorium in Vence, France (February); dies in village (March 2).

Notes on the Editor and Contributors

MARK KINKEAD-WEEKES is Senior Lecturer in English at the University of Kent at Canterbury and coauthor of *William Golding: A Critical Study* (1967).

H. M. DALESKI is a member of the English Faculty at the Hebrew University of Jerusalem.

GEORGE H. FORD, Professor and Chairman of the Department of English at the University of Rochester, is author of *Keats and the Victorians* (1962) and *Dickens and His Readers* (1965). He is also one of the editors of the *Norton Anthology of English Literature*.

LAURENCE LERNER is Professor of English at the University of Sussex; author of *The Truest Poetry* (1960), several volumes of poetry, and a novel; and coauthor of collections of contemporary reviews of George Eliot and Thomas Hardy.

MARVIN MUDRICK, Professor of English at the University of California, Santa Barbara, is the author of *Jane Austen: Irony as Defense and Discovery* (1952) and a study of Colette. He edited *Conrad: A Collection of Critical Essays* in the Twentieth Century Views series.

KEITH SAGAR is Staff Tutor in the Extra-Mural Department of the University of Manchester.

WILLIAM WALSH is Professor of Education at the University of Leeds and author of *A Human Idiom: Literature and Humanity* (1964) and *Coleridge* (1967).

Selected Bibliography

This collection should have begun, as definitive criticism of Lawrence did, with a selection from F. R. Leavis' *D. H. Lawrence: Novelist*, Chatto and Windus, 1955; but Dr. Leavis was unwilling to grant permission. His chapter on *The Rainbow*, "Lawrence and Tradition" should be read in conjunction with Marvin Mudrick's rejoinder, printed here—and, indeed, with Eugene Goodheart, *The Utopian Vision of D. H. Lawrence*, University of Chicago Press, 1963, who sets him in the "Tradition" of Blake and Nietzsche. Several books which followed Leavis' pioneering study contain valuable insight: Mark Spilka, *The Love Ethic of D. H. Lawrence*, Indiana University Press, 1955; Graham Hough, *The Dark Sun*, Duckworth, 1957; Eliseo Vivas, *D. H. Lawrence: The Failure and the Triumph of Art*, Northwestern University Press, 1960; Julian Moynahan, *The Deed of Life*, Princeton, 1963. S. L. Goldberg's essay "The Rainbow: Fiddle-bow and Sand," *Essays in Criticism* 11 (October 1961), which I should have liked to reprint, poses the major critical problem cogently.

There have recently been important advances in the study of Lawrence by several authors represented in this collection. H. M. Daleski in *The Forked Flame*, Faber, 1965, first established the significance of the *Study of Thomas Hardy*. Keith Sagar's *The Art of D. H. Lawrence*, Cambridge, 1966, suggests the importance of seeing Lawrence's novels in the context of his other work at the time (the chronological tables and bibliography will be found extremely useful). George H. Ford, to whom I owe a personal debt of gratitude, has shown the value of work on Lawrence's manuscripts, in his publication of cancelled chapters of *Women in Love*, and in his *Double Measure*, Holt, Rinehart and Winston, 1965. Recently Colin Clarke, in his *River of Dissolution*, Routledge and Kegan Paul, 1969, has contributed a valuable study of Lawrence's treatment of "corruption."

For Lawrence's life, see Edward Nehls's invaluable compilation of memoirs, *D. H. Lawrence: A Composite Biography*, University of Wisconsin, 1957; and the single-volume study by Harry T. Moore, *The Intelligent Heart*, Heinemann, 1955 (reprinted by Penguin Books, 1960). Mark Spilka's Introduction to *D. H. Lawrence: A Collection of Critical Essays*, Prentice-Hall, 1963, is a good survey of the development of criticism of Lawrence. R. P. Draper's collection in the "Critical Heritage" series, Routledge and Kegan Paul, is forthcoming.